LAW, CRIME AND LAW ENFORCEMENT

ADVANCES IN CRIMINOLOGY RESEARCH

LAW, CRIME AND LAW ENFORCEMENT

Additional books in this series can be found on Nova's website under the Series tab.

Additional e-books in this series can be found on Nova's website under the e-book tab.

LAW, CRIME AND LAW ENFORCEMENT

ADVANCES IN CRIMINOLOGY RESEARCH

JULIA GUZMAN
EDITOR

nova publishers
New York

NOTICE TO THE READER

Library of Congress Cataloging-in-Publication Data

Advances in criminology research / editor, Julia Guzman.
pages cm. -- (Law, crime and law enforcement)
Includes index.
ISBN 978-1-63483-180-2 (hardcover)
1. Criminology--Research. 2. Criminology. I. Guzman, Julia, 1972-
HV6024.5.A35 2015
364.072--dc23
2015021920

Published by Nova Science Publishers, Inc. † New York

CONTENTS

Preface **vii**

Chapter 1 Spatial Analysis of Causes of Criminality: Theoretical Background, Methodology, Implementation Experience **1**
Dmitry V. Bakharev

Chapter 2 Integrated Criminology and Biological Related Criminology Facing White Collar Crime **41**
Tage Alalehto

Chapter 3 Categorization, Stereotyping, Status and Police Traffic Stop Behavior **73**
Christopher Barnum, Michael Lovaglia and Jared Miller

Chapter 4 Can Differences in Attachment to Parents and Level of Self-Control Explain the Gender Gap in Juvenile Delinquency? Testing a Gendered Attachment–Self-Control Theory **91**
Helmut Hirtenlehner and Brenda Sims Blackwell

Index **117**

PREFACE

In this book, the authors discuss recent advances in criminology research. In the first chapter, the author gives a spatial analysis of the causes of criminality. Spatial analysis is one of the most widespread methods of criminological research in English-speaking countries, where It is applied for the identification of the reasons of individual criminal behavior. The author of the chapter suggests that spatial analysis also can be applied to study the reasons of crime. In the second chapter, the author provides a combination of integrated and biosocial approaches on criminology. This chapter provides an argument whereby the agenda of white collar crime research can be developed by a synthesis of integrated and biosocial factors. In the third chapter, the authors present a theory that describes the association between social categories and inequitable police enforcement behavior. The social sciences have long been interested in the ways that an individual's demographic characteristics such as race, gender and age shape behavior in applied settings where people differ in power and status. In the last chapter, the gendered attachment-self-control theory is examined, designed to explain the gender differences in criminal involvement.

Chapter 1 – Spatial analysis is one of the most widespread methods of criminological research in English-speaking countries. It is applied for the identification of the reasons of individual criminal behavior and for the determination of separate categories of crimes (for example, violent, sexual, against property, etc.). This method, as a rule, is realized in the following manner: 1) topographic linkage of places where crimes have been committed; 2) discovery of the "hot spots" of criminality, i.e., spatially determined areas with the highest density of crimes committed; 3) analysis of the socio-economic structure of districts within which there are concentrations of "hot spots" of criminality; and 4) empirical (statistical) checking of the interconnection of structural aspects of 'districts with criminality' and the level and quality of social control in them. Meanwhile, in Russian scientific research on the given issue, as a rule, territorial systems at the regional level predominate as the subject for study.

The analysis of distinctions of indicators of crime in regions has the purpose of identification of the reason of crime as a social phenomenon. Moreover, the common algorithm for studying the causes of territorial differences of criminality is the following: 1) using the comparative method, one reveals the peculiarities of socio-economic development of regional systems from the point of view of a broad spectrum of criteria; 2) this information is compared (including with the help of methods of correlation and regression analysis) with data about the level, condition and trend line of criminality in the regions under review; 3) we highlight the specific tendencies driving the behavior of socio-economic processes in the region that are interrelated (positively or negatively) with the trend line of criminality figures in them (for example, the level and speed of development of the economic sphere of the regions are usually inversely correlated with the level and trend line of criminality); and 4) on the basis of analysis of these positive and negative tendencies applicable to the concrete region, one may forecast the change in criminality figures there.

At the same time, in the framework of the given scheme of research, there are still a range of contradictions observed in the sphere of recorded criminality in the Russian regions during the first half of the 2000s that remain unresolved. Thus, for example, during this period, a high level of criminality was observed in the Eastern regions of the country, where there was a weak, resource-oriented economy and a significant share of rural population in decline (Republic of Buryatia, Transbaikal region, Irkutsk Region, Kurgan Region and a number of others), and in regions with the opposite socio-economic profile, such as the industrially developed and highly urbanized territories of the Urals-Perm district and the Sverdlovsk oblast. However, among the regions gravitating towards the 'positive' pole of tendencies of criminality, there were in this period of time also the least developed republics in terms of socio-economics, such as the Northern Caucasus and, on the contrary, the territories of the Center and South of Russia - the Krasnodar region, Belgorod and Voronezh Regions, among other, with their dynamic development in this sense.

The author believes that key to the specified contradictions is the spatial analysis of the reasons of crime - the new approach in criminological research that is based on Spatial Economy and "New Economic Geography." In the present chapter, the theoretical prerequisites and methodology as well as the results of realization of the similar research that was carried out on the example of regions of Central Federal District of the Russian Federation are presented.

Chapter 2 – During the last two decades the rise of integrated approaches and biosocial approaches has given criminology a fresh theoretical and empirical approach. However, a full scale integration of these two approaches has not come to a conclusion over the etiological question of what forms the criminal mind. The aim of this article is to give an argument whereby the agenda of white collar crime research can be developed by a synthesis of integrated and biosocial factors. The argument takes its standpoint in one of the recent theories on white collar crime research today, the crime-as-choice theory. The theory proposes an integrated model of factors working on different levels. For example, the linkage between lacks of credible oversight on aggregated level, the existence of a crime-facilitative culture on organizational level, and propensities towards aggressiveness, thrill-seeking, resilience, and entitlement on individual level. However, as a typical social scientific theory the crime-as-choice theory lacks a complete etiological argument behind its proposed proximate causality. I elaborate upon the etiological concepts from the fields of evolutionary theory and institutional theory how the crime-as-choice theory can get an even more coherent structure between ultimate and proximate causes.

Chapter 3 – The social sciences have long been interested in the ways that an individual's demographic characteristics such as race, gender and age shape behavior in applied settings where people differ in power and status. In recent years this interest has been fueled by high profile news stories about mistreatment of segments of the population at the hands of powerful actors. Research on police bias for example, has found that minority members are often overrepresented in police-citizen encounters including stops and arrests. These findings are consistent across a broad range of research methodologies and wide variety of law enforcement agencies. While the overall conclusion from these studies is clear—the police to varying degrees tend to disproportionately stop or sanction minority members—the reasons for disproportionality are less evident. Recent theorizing has proffered a number of explanations for the sources of disparity. These include status differences between the police and minority members, police perceptions of criminal activity in an area, social psychological processes, implicit cognitive bias, econometric models as well as racial profiling and directed patrol.

Chapter 4 – That boys are more likely to offend than girls is a well-established finding in contemporary criminology; however, few theoretical perspectives directly focus on explaining this gap. In 2002, Hayslett-McCall and Bernard introduced a new perspective, the gendered attachment–self-control theory, designed to explain the gender difference in criminal involvement. The theory posits that boys experience more disruptions in early attachments to primary caregivers, which leads to them developing less self-control and, consequently, a higher propensity to offend. This study assesses this perspective, which to date has been empirically neglected, using survey data from Austria. With boys reporting more crime and lower levels of both self-control and attachment to the mother than girls, and strong attachment to the mother being linked to weak self-control as well as low self-control predicting criminal behavior, the results provide some support for the theory.

In: Advances in Criminology Research
Editor: Julia Guzman
ISBN: 978-1-63483-180-2

Chapter 1

SPATIAL ANALYSIS OF CAUSES OF CRIMINALITY: THEORETICAL BACKGROUND, METHODOLOGY, IMPLEMENTATION EXPERIENCE

Dmitry V. Bakharev
Department of economics and law, Surgut
State Pedagogical University, Surgut, Russia

ABSTRACT

Spatial analysis is one of the most widespread methods of criminological research in English-speaking countries. It is applied for the identification of the reasons of individual criminal behavior and for the determination of separate categories of crimes (for example, violent, sexual, against property, etc.). This method, as a rule, is realized in the following manner: 1) topographic linkage of places where crimes have been committed; 2) discovery of the "hot spots" of criminality, i.e., spatially determined areas with the highest density of crimes committed; 3) analysis of the socio-economic structure of districts within which there are concentrations of "hot spots" of criminality; and 4) empirical (statistical) checking of the interconnection of structural aspects of 'districts with criminality' and the level and quality of social control in them. Meanwhile, in Russian scientific research on the given issue, as a rule, territorial systems at the regional level predominate as the subject for study.

The analysis of distinctions of indicators of crime in regions has the purpose of identification of the reason of crime as a social phenomenon. Moreover, the common algorithm for studying the causes of territorial differences of criminality is the following: 1) using the comparative method, one reveals the peculiarities of socio-economic development of regional systems from the point of view of a broad spectrum of criteria; 2) this information is compared (including with the help of methods of correlation and regression analysis) with data about the level, condition and trend line of criminality in the regions under review; 3) we highlight the specific tendencies driving the behavior of socio-economic processes in the region that are interrelated (positively or negatively) with the trend line of criminality figures in them (for example, the level and speed of development of the economic sphere of the regions are usually inversely correlated with the level and trend line of criminality); and 4) on the basis of analysis of these positive and negative tendencies applicable to the concrete region, one may forecast the change in criminality figures there.

At the same time, in the framework of the given scheme of research, there are still a range of contradictions observed in the sphere of recorded criminality in the Russian regions during the first half of the 2000s that remain unresolved. Thus, for example, during this period, a high level of criminality was observed in the Eastern regions of the country, where there was a weak, resource-oriented economy and a significant share of rural population in decline (Republic of Buryatia, Transbaikal region, Irkutsk Region, Kurgan Region and a number of others), and in regions with the opposite socio-economic profile, such as the industrially developed and highly urbanized territories of the Urals-Perm district and the Sverdlovsk oblast. However, among the regions gravitating towards the 'positive' pole of tendencies of criminality, there were in this period of time also the least developed republics in terms of socio-economics, such as the Northern Caucasus and, on the contrary, the territories of the Center and South of Russia - the Krasnodar region, Belgorod and Voronezh Regions, among other, with their dynamic development in this sense.

The author believes that key to the specified contradictions is the spatial analysis of the reasons of crime - the new approach in criminological research that is based on Spatial Economy and "New Economic Geography." In the present chapter, the theoretical prerequisites and methodology as well as the results of realization of the similar research that was carried out on the example of regions of Central Federal District of the Russian Federation are presented.

INTRODUCTION

Study of causes of criminality in territorial aspects is the first and, at the same time, the most comprehensive approach to criminological research, combining a significant number of methods of scientific comprehension. The core of the developed *territorial approach*, in broad lines, can be quintessentialized as follows. It is applied to examine factors (causes) of criminality and consists of a) analysis and comparison of criminal activeness of the population of certain territorial systems of various levels (city, village, district, region, separate country) and b) identification of particular (economic, social, demographic, cultural, etc.) factors manifested in a specific way within these territorial systems and finding the interrelation of the above factors with criminality indicators in these areas. Upon the establishment of certain interrelation of changes in indicators within a particular area and observed deviation of individual indicators characterizing various aspects of the life of its population, we conclude that it was those deviations that were the causes of increased activeness of people in the criminal sphere.

The practice of implementation of the territorial approach by Soviet criminologists enabled proving of the thesis that criminality is a social phenomenon because all changes occurring thereto are driven by the nature of transformation of social processes as a whole. The correlation of multiannual and rather broad-ranging empirical studies of criminality indicators with statistical data characterizing particular social life aspects, carried out in relation to inhabited localities or administrative-territorial units of other level, confirmed the hypothesis of the social nature and structure of causes of criminality [1, 2, 14].

Under the conditions of the administrative-command system and centrally planned economy that existed in the USSR, these scientific conclusions were of very serious significance for the practice as a whole. The overall long-term planning of development in almost all spheres of life of the Soviet society made it possible to predict – in advance and with a high degree of probability – the criminologically significant consequences of the measures of socioeconomic nature that were intended to be implemented by the machinery of party and government in a given region of the country. Therefore, already at the planning stage, the specialists had an opportunity to give a reasonable forecast of criminogenic processes development in this territory and to work out a program for prevention of increase in crime therein.

Moreover, in the second half of the 1980s, leading Soviet criminologists noted that, with such presentation of an issue, the problem of causes of criminality is reduced only to finding, in particular conditions of the territory under investigation, what exact reason gives rise to criminality, from what sphere of the people's social life its roots derive. Thus, if the problem is viewed only from this perspective, the most natural way to address it is through meticulous study of all possible correlations between the totality of crimes (or criminals), on the one hand, and various spheres of social life, on the other hand. The points where the correlation relationships are the strongest hide in themselves the key, determinant causes of criminality [8, 23]. However, against the background of the serious theoretical progress in understanding the essence of crime (which, like any social phenomenon, being one of the characteristics of the social organism state, is determined by the totality of socioeconomic, political, and other factors, with this totality affecting the criminality not through its individual elements, but in an integrated way, through the whole system of factors interacting with each other [13, 9]), a gnoseological limitation of the territorial approach became apparent with such a definition of the former's objectives.

Considering this circumstance, it was assumed that the territorial approach to comprehension of causes of criminality may be the most fruitful (with such understanding of the criminality essence) in the case when the approach consists of the criminological analysis of functioning of territorial/spatial systems as well as finding destabilizing factors, sources of disorganization, and social tension therein. Accordingly, the primary focus should not be on individual fragments of social reality, nor on the study of processes and phenomena taken out of the integral social organism, in their interaction with criminality, but only on something qualitatively new that is discovered as a result of the overall interaction and mutual influence of all key components and spheres of the social system under consideration [8, 2-29]. However, it was at that point in time when quite a number of questions of theoretical nature arose that, unless resolved, made implementation of the territorial approach based on a similar conceptual platform not only dilemmatic but virtually impossible.

In particular, Soviet experts focused on the fact that the process of comprehension of the functioning of complex social systems, which include territorial/spatial systems of regional and community levels, should be implemented on a dynamic basis because the changes occurring therein have not been caused by a significant impact just rendered on them but rather have been mediated by the whole chain of impacts and response reactions of the system over the past period of time. Therefore, it is necessary to know which factors determine the dynamic behavior of complex systems, and hence, criminology was faced with a task of developing methods to quantitatively analyze the dynamic behavior of complex systems, the interaction of which forms the causal socioeconomic complex of criminality [13, 16-18]. However, it should be stated that at the present time, the process of solving this problem not only by criminology but by the totality of sciences of the social cycle is still very far from its completion. At the same time, this problem is far from having lost its relevance, but, on the contrary, the results of its solution are critically important for further progress in comprehension of the mechanism of criminality determination through the territorial approach.

It seems that modern researchers of this problem should refer to the achievements of the regional economy and the socioeconomic geography at the junction of which a new interdisciplinary field of socioeconomic processes study from the territorial (spatial) perspective – spatial economics – is currently being formed. Its objectives can generally be formulated as follows: identifying laws and patterns of socioeconomic processes in space, and building, on this basis, forecasts of development thereof on short- and long-term horizons. Within the framework of spatial economics, subject to comprehensive analysis are almost all socioeconomic phenomena that criminologists have been long interested in (in the context of comparing them with criminality indicators): the settlement system, urbanization and migration processes, the branch structure of economy of a certain region, the level and quality of its inhabitants' lives, and others.

Taking as a basis the initial pattern of these processes in regions of the country, fixed on the map, representatives of spatial economy undertake attempts, first, to understand the laws of formation of this pattern in conditions of today's market – not the previous planned-economy – i.e., under natural (free) variation of factors of production and goods, and, second, to predict the mechanism for implementing the identified laws in the future and for their reflection from the spatial perspective.

Analysis of the research results in this sphere suggests that the development of socioeconomic processes in the framework of regional systems at the present stage of history is characterized by the existence of the following laws:

1. the role of the driving force for socioeconomic development of individual territorial systems in modern conditions is fulfilled by large cities – economic centers in the form of agglomerations. For even development of the country's territory, the distribution of large cities should be sufficiently uniform and dense. Population density is also

important for the settlement system: the higher the former is, the higher is the capacity of the consumer market and the lower are transport costs for the end product delivery [3, 4, 5]; therefore, the economy of the region grows more rapidly. Demographic indicators most closely and fully correlate with the overall "life climate" formed in the area or inhabited locality under investigation. The higher is the size and density of population of a certain city, the brisker is the development of economic, cultural, creative, and other positive activities of its citizens. A city becomes a "growth point," an organizing element for the development of the "center-periphery" processes, and, due to "diffusion of innovations," exerts positive effect on development of the surrounding territory and, consequently, the whole region. As a result, the degree of attractiveness of the regional socioeconomic environment begins to be appreciated not only by its inhabitants but also by the population of the neighboring (and other) areas;

2. other factors that ensure "successfulness" of development of the regional socioeconomic systems are the following: sufficiently developed infrastructure (first of all, transport arteries); attractiveness of the territory from the viewpoint of inhabitants of other regions of the country and foreigners (the territory should also have a positive migration balance); and the extensiveness of the economic base of the region (including the resource potential and production base);
3. therefore, the "starting" conditions for the development of regions are determined, generally, by the existence and manifestation degree of these basic factors of socioeconomic development. In addition, a significant impact on the rate and the vector of such development itself is exerted by the specific nature of the established institutional environment of the region (quality of activity of administrative and managerial machinery, the overall business climate, etc.) and by the presence and nature (positive or negative) of external influencing factors, such as "neighborhoods" with socioeconomically depressive territories or, on the contrary, with strong leaders in this regard.

Under the current Russian conditions, the abovementioned positive processes are almost always accompanied by negative consequences in the form of the following: a) the depopulation of the territory; b) the decrease in intensity of its economic use; c) the reduction of quality of human capital in the areas being depopulated; and d) the deterioration in the quality of the territorial infrastructure, among others. As a whole, this process was named "social space shrinkage." As a result, the degree of successful socioeconomic development of a given territory, estimated based on analysis of data on the level and dynamics of economic development of the region, the rate of reproduction of its demographic base, and quality of its population's health, as well as quality of the population as a whole (educational level etc.), is defined, on the one hand, by the vector and intensity of the "center-periphery" processes and, on the other hand, by specific features of the social space shrinkage manifestation.

Theoretically, the most favorable situation in socioeconomic terms, which is expressed in relatively higher growth of these factors, develops in those regional systems where the tendencies of shrinkage of socially utilized space manifest themselves to the least degree, while positive urbanization and migration processes are, on the contrary, the most active.

Hence, in terms of testing the above hypothesis regarding the laws of development of the region as a complex system, it is of interest to consider the totality of socioeconomic phenomena and processes, including criminality, no longer in the territorial but already in the *spatial* aspect, which implies the following: a) the initial selection of territorial systems, where development of socioeconomic processes is subject to common laws, which manifests itself in the existence of similar trends in such development; b) the overall assessment of the territories selected for analysis from the viewpoint of their socioeconomic attractiveness for living; identification of the territories that are leaders or outsiders in terms of human capital reproduction, accumulation, and attraction, of deepening and expanding their economic base, of improving the qualitative characteristics of their population itself and classification of the above territories according to the acuteness of the problem of their social space shrinkage; and c) comparison of this information with the data on criminality level, state, and dynamics in the territorial systems under consideration.

Specific techniques for implementing the above general methodological scheme of spatial analysis of causes of criminality include the following steps:

- identification of territorial socioeconomic systems of different levels, within which it is possible to collect and analyze information on manifestations of criminal activeness of the population of these territories;
- breakdown of the territorial unit (for example, cities or regions) array selected for the analysis into separate typological groups. The classification criterion in this case is the existence of the common

laws of socioeconomic processes development. The territorial systems belonging to the same typological group have to make a unified, in this respect, socioeconomic space: the dynamics and vector of development of all parts of this space are to be determined by the same factors in terms of the theory of the "center-periphery" relations;

- further, based on the estimation of the existence and degree of manifestation of these basic factors of socioeconomic development, in each typological group, social and territorial units that are potential leaders or outsiders in terms of prospects for such development should be identified;
- the next step is analysis of the rates and dynamics of socioeconomic development of these territorial socioeconomic systems. The number of integral characteristics of this development has a clear tendency to increase and even now includes the following: the level and dynamics of economic development of the territory, quality of life of the population, and quality of human capital of the territory, as well as a number of other indicators. Individually, within each typological group of territories, it is possible to study existing imbalances in their socioeconomic development;
- further evaluation of the results of socioeconomic development of the territorial systems based on the prospects for such a development that they initially had are implemented: comparison of the potential and the degree of its actualization is carried out;
- the subsequent step is the selection of statistical indicators that most fully and comprehensively characterize the state of criminality within each territorial system included into the obtained typological groups. The array of these indicators traditionally include the criminality level, structure, and dynamics (absolute values of the criminality indicators (extremum points), as well as periods of their growth, decline, stabilization, and the rates of these changes);
- in addition, the analysis of these indicators for each territorial unit selected for the analysis and included into a certain typological group is implemented;
- subsequently, data on the prospects, dynamics, and results of economic and social development of territorial units of the identified typological groups with the discovered trends and patterns of criminality therein are compared;

– the final step is the analysis of the obtained results and a statement of conclusions.

It appears that testing the proposed scheme of application of the spatial approach to the analysis of causes of criminality should be carried out by taking territorial socioeconomic systems at the regional level (subjects of the Russian Federation) as a subject of analysis: currently, all the necessary statistical information is publicly available only for these systems.

Upon breakdown of the totality of regions into individual typological groups in terms of manifestation of common patterns of socioeconomic development in these regions, and after selection of certain groups for the analysis, it is necessary to perform estimation of their constituent regions in terms of a) existence and b) degree of manifestation of other basic socioeconomic development factors. Among these factors, the following should be considered: 1) population density of the region; 2) urban population share; 3) population migration balance (outflow and inflow of the region inhabitants); 4) the region's infrastructure development degree; 5) the number of urban agglomerations; and 6) the region's economic base development degree.

The time period for which all the data will be analyzed is reasonably defined as eleven years, from 2003 to 2013. The indicator of population density should be the total population of the region (pers.) in 2003 divided by the area of the region (km^2). The urban population share is calculated as the ratio of the urban settlement population size to the total population size of the region (pers.). The region's population migration balance is the total number of inhabitants who arrived in / left the region from 2003 to 2013. As an indicator of the region's infrastructure development degree, it is quite adequate to use data on the density of general use of hard-surface roads (km) per thousand kilometers. The presence and the number of urban agglomerations in the region are determined in accordance with generally accepted criteria of these concepts and with expert evaluations by specialists on the subject. Finally, the economic base is estimated on the basis of the current sectoral structure of gross regional product of the region (dominant sectors of industry should be pointed out) [10, 12].

The obtained typological arrays of territorial units should be analyzed from the standpoint of determining the value and dynamics of indicators characterizing the results of life activities of population of these territories in the socioeconomic aspect, as well as of indicators characterizing the quality of the population itself.

In this sense, it seems expedient to select three groups of indicators illustrating the following: a) the level and dynamics of economic development of the region, the success of which is, to a considerable degree, the base for b) reproduction of the region's demographic base and improvement of the population's health quality, and the base for c) improvement of the region's population quality. Among the indicators characterizing the economic situation of the region to the fullest and most comprehensive extent, the annual gross regional product as well as the amount of investments in fixed assets (in rubles per capita) should be considered. Among the second group indicators, the following data describing the demographic situation and state of the population's health should be considered: the rate of natural increase (decrease) of the population (the difference between total mortality and birth rate, per thousand of the population), life expectancy (the number of years collectively for men and women), and infant mortality rate (the number of infants who died before the age of 1 year per 1,000 live births). As a generalized characteristic of the population quality, the following indicator of educational level composed, in turn, of three factors, should be considered: a) the share of persons with science degrees (pers.) in relation to the average annual number of people employed in the economy (thousand pers.); b) share of persons with higher education in relation to the average annual number of people employed in the economy (pers.); and c) share of persons with post-graduate education in relation to the average annual number of people employed in the economy (pers.). Due to the fact that the official statistics record the educational level of each individual employable person only within the framework of population censuses (conducted no more often than once every 8-10 years), to calculate these three indicators, one should use the data on the number of persons having a certain level of education published on the websites of the Russian National Population Census of 2002 and 2010 [6, 7], whereas the information on the average annual number of people employed in the economy should be taken from the digests "Russian Regions. Socioeconomic Indicators," for 2003 and 2011 [10, 11].

Further, using the method of *sum of places*, the position of each region in its group is determined by the indicators characterizing the demographic situation, state of health and educational level of the population, within the initial (2002) and the final (2010 or 2013) periods. The indicators of natural increase rate, life expectancy, and the three indicators characterizing the population's educational level act as incentives, i.e., their increase has a positive impact on the overall state of the region. In contrast, the rate of infant mortality is a disincentive because its increase acts as an adverse factor.

Regions are ranked by the incentive indicators in ascending order and by the disincentive indicators in descending order. For each region, the places taken by it are summed up during consideration of each indicator. In accordance with the sum of places gained by each region, the final ranking of the latter is performed. The number of places (ranks) is equal to the number of the subjects under consideration. Thus, places in the groups are distributed from the 1st to the 6th: the smaller is the sum of places gained by each region, the higher is the rank assigned to it.

The general algorithm for the method of sum of places can be expressed by the following formula:

$$R_{ij} = \sum_{i=1}^{n} p_{ij}; j = \overline{1,m} \quad (1.1)$$

where is the place of the jth region by the ith indicator.

By analyzing the difference in the ranks and places of regions by each of the analyzed indicators within the initial and final periods, the existence of the dynamics (positive or negative) or its absence is determined, for both each individual indicator and a group of indicators as a whole.

The most relevant group of regions in terms of the existence of common patterns of socioeconomic development are, in our opinion, the subjects of the Central Federal District (CFD): they are relatively similar in terms of basic socioeconomic conditions of their life activity; are located in approximately the same natural and climatic conditions; have comparable production and infrastructure bases, similar settlement system and age pattern of the inhabitants; and are all, in varying degree, affected by the positive-negative influence of the city of Moscow and the Moscow Region, which, in terms of all their characteristics, is in a marked contrast to all the other subjects of the Central Federal District. In addition, some regions feature an increased share of urban population in 2003 (over 75%) "rising above" the other regions: the Vladimir, Ivanovo, Tula and Yaroslavl Regions. As a result, twelve regions of the Central Federal District were chosen as subjects of study: Belgorod, Bryansk, Voronezh, Kaluga, Kostroma, Kursk, Lipetsk, Oryol, Ryazan, Smolensk, Tambov and Tver Regions.

Initially, the twelve regions of the Central Federal District can be divided into two typological groups – with more or less favorable economic situation and geographic position.

Figure 1. Administrative-territorial division of the Central Federal District.

Based on the above criterion, the first group should include the following Regions: Belgorod (the Central Black Earth Region, bordered by densely populated industrial regions of Eastern Ukraine), Voronezh (with similar characteristics), Kursk, Lipetsk (the Central Black Earth Region), Smolensk (transport and infrastructure corridors in the directions of "Moscow – Minsk – Western Europe" and "St. Petersburg – the South of Russia and Ukraine"; prospects for development of customs infrastructure on the border with Belarus), and Tver (the transport corridor between the country's largest agglomerations – those of Moscow and St. Petersburg). The second group should include five regions of the non-Black Earth area (Bryansk, Kaluga, Kostroma, Oryol, Ryazan Regions), as well as the Black Earth Tambov Region, whose peripheral nature and infrastructure limitation significantly restrict this natural strength. In terms of the presence and degree of manifestation of basic socioeconomic development factors in the regions of the first group (see Table 1), the leader is obvious: it is the Belgorod Region. In addition to the high figures characterizing the settlement network, the population itself, as well as the quality of infrastructure (exceeding the average values of these parameters in the whole group), this subject of the Federation compares favorably with its group-mates by having two (though not large) agglomerations located in different parts of the region, as well as by having developed agriculture and export-oriented economic sectors.

Table 1. Coverage of the first group's regions with basic socioeconomic development factors

	Population density	Roadway network development degree	Urban population share	Migration balance	Presence of agglomerations	Structure of economy
Belgorod Region	55.3	241	66%	663	2	High share of industry (iron and steel industry) and agriculture
Voronezh Region	45.7	175	62%	485	1 (million)	Low share of industry and high share of agriculture
Kursk Region	42.6	206	61.20%	-110	-	Low share of industry (machine-building, chemical, iron ore extraction industries) and high share of agriculture
Lipetsk Region	50.6	216	64.30%	190	-	High share of industry (iron and steel industry) and low share of agriculture
Smolensk Region	21.8	178	71%	152	-	Significant share of industry (manufacturing activities) and increased, for the non-Black Earth area, share of agriculture
Tver Region	18.2	178	73%	84	-	Significant share of industry (fabric and machine-building industries) and increased, for the non-Black Earth area, share of agriculture
Group average	29.8	199	66.33	244		

The second place can be shared by the Voronezh and Lipetsk Regions. The former is distinguished by presence of almost a million agglomeration and a high positive migration balance and the latter by a very large share of iron and steel industry in the economy, the products of which are mainly exported. Regarding the obvious disadvantage, in terms of the regional economy development stability, in relation to the Voronezh Region, it is the insufficient degree of development of export-oriented industrial production, which, as a rule, acts as the driving force of agrarian regional development [8].

The following is the Kursk Region. With its lack of a highly developed production base meeting the requirements of the present-day market conditions, this region, however, has a sufficient density of population and a well-developed roadway network. Finally, the group's "outsiders" are the Smolensk and Tver Regions. All the characteristics of these regions demonstrate that they have very little chance to maintain a respectable level of socioeconomic development against the background of their group-mates. Actually, there is only one chance for both regions, and it consists of making maximum use of the benefits of their transit-oriented location for development of the so-called "tertiary sector," i.e., the service sector oriented to the carriers and passengers travelling around the territory of these regions in large numbers.

Examining the status of coverage of the second group's six regions with basic socioeconomic development factors (see Table 2), one can note that the pattern is much more "blurred" than that of the first group's regions – both obvious leaders and potential outsiders are more difficult to identify here. However, the situation of the Kaluga Region seems to be the most favorable in this respect. This subject of the Federation has a favorable geographic position in relation to the Moscow Region, a high share of urban population, a well-developed transport network, and a large urban agglomeration.

At the same time, this region is focused on the machine-building industry, i.e., it is in a knowingly loss-making situation in relation to its group-mates that have more profitable industrial sectors in terms of exporting their products. However, even this drawback, as will be shown later, will, in combination with the above positive factors, turn into an advantage and affect formation of the vector of further economic development of Kaluga Region.

Bryansk Region is characterized by a much lower chance of success in terms of economic development. It was seriously affected as a result of the accident at the Chernobyl nuclear power plant, whereby the migration outflow from this region remains significant.

Table 2. Coverage of the second group's regions with basic socioeconomic development factors

	Population density	Roadway network development degree	Urban population share	Migration balance	Presence of agglomerations	Structure of economy
Bryansk Region	40	184	68.5%	-136	1	Low share of industry (machine-building industry) and high share of agriculture
Kaluga Region	35.1	172	75%	342	1	Significant share of industry (machine-building industry) and increased, for the non-Black Earth area, share of agriculture
Kostroma Region	12.6	93	67.3%	-243		Decreased share of industry (timber and woodworking, machine-building industries) and high share of agriculture
Oryol Region	35.5	168	62%	-149		Low share of industry (machine-building and food industries) and high share of agriculture

Table 2. (Continued)

	Population density	Roadway network development degree	Urban population share	Migration balance	Presence of agglomerations	Structure of economy
Ryazan Region	31.3	171	68.9%	214		Low share of industry (energy producing and oil refining industries) and increased, for the non-Black Earth area, share of agriculture
Tambov Region	35.7	160	57.3%	-35		Low share of industry (food industry) and high share of agriculture
Group average	31.7	158	66.5%	-1.16		

On the contrary, the Ryazan Region, comparable to the Bryansk Region in many respects, located closer to Moscow and having a more favorable industrial structure, acts as the migration "recipient." As for the Oryol Region, it comes short even of these small benefits. Although it has a fairly extensive area of black soil lands, the forecast of its development is also more likely to be unfavorable.

An obvious outsider of the second group of regions, in terms of socioeconomic development factors, is Kostroma Region. Its geographic position is the most unfavorable of all the second group's regions. The Volga River actually divides it into two parts: the smaller and relatively developed one (on the left bank) and the larger one, which is not fully developed in socioeconomic terms (the right bank of the Volga); as for the bridges connecting the two parts of the region, they are very few in number.

With regard to Tambov Region, despite the lack of a sufficient degree of basic socioeconomic development factors, it is the Black Earth region. As a result, historically, the most favorable structure of rural settlements (typical for the Black Earth area as a whole) has formed in this region, compared with all other regions of the second group: one rural inhabited locality per 19.56 km^2. In addition, urban settlements, the centers for the surrounding rural areas, are evenly distributed throughout the region territory.

In addition, the enterprises of the food industry, which dominate in Tambov Region, are located in the region's towns in a relatively balanced manner. Thus, agriculture (being, moreover, sufficiently provided with social and industrial infrastructures), which is well-developed in this region, has a realistic chance to act as a kind of a "lifebuoy" for the Tambov region, which is exposed to serious threats in the economic and social spheres.

We now consider the dynamics of the gross regional product and amount of investments in the regions of this group over a period from 2003 to 2013 (see Tables 3, 4).

Thus, it is obvious that the regions of the group under consideration, which were characterized by the most favorable combination of socioeconomic development factors, i.e., initially had the greatest chance to form the required vector for development of their economy, were quite able to implement the opportunities that they had, and, in this respect, they left their group-mates behind. To a greater extent, this was typical for Belgorod Region, and to a much lesser extent for Lipetsk Region.

Significantly inferior to Belgorod Region in terms of the urban population share, migration balance, and the degree of diversity of the sectoral structure of the economy, Lipetsk Region experienced a tangible decrease in the rate of growth of its economy in 2009-2012.

Disturbing signs of a slowing rate of economic growth in 2012-2013 also began to manifest themselves in Belgorod Region. A curious situation is in Voronezh Region: this agrarian region with a low share and unfavorable structure of industrial production proved to be able to quite successfully make use of its "genetic" benefits represented by an advantageous structure of rural settlement network, relatively well-developed roadway network, and the Voronezh agglomeration, which is the largest one in the Central Federal District, and significantly improved the situation of its economic sphere. However, it is to be recalled that the positive trends have vividly demonstrated themselves only since 2010. Prior to that, the natural advantages of Voronezh Region (in terms of spatial development patterns) were not used to the full. Kursk Region – an "average performer" – has retained, to a considerable extent, its mid position also in terms of economic development.

Table 3. Gross regional product per capita in the first group's regions (thousand rubles)

	2003	2004	2005	2006	2007	2008	2009	2010	2011	2012
Belgorod Region	50284.0	75650.0	95911.2	118211.4	156225.1	208548.1	199046.1	260015.6	331010.0	354982.9
Voronezh Region	42361.8	50003.5	56534.5	70492.7	94849.5	122591.1	129112.5	148432.6	203575.5	243941.3
Kursk Region	46109.9	63396.2	72995.3	88949.4	111348.4	146276.4	141833.5	171322.1	203676.0	226551.7
Lipetsk Region	79802.6	118602.3	121376.2	150197.1	176534.6	219135.8	192165.2	211610.6	246213.8	253302.1
Smolensk Region	47238.6	54706.5	63687.0	77366.8	94432.4	121012.7	125743.1	156567.3	184184.9	205874.5
Tver Region	47301.9	61396.6	68048.7	90517.8	112021.5	139216.2	144257.9	161305.0	189484.3	200009.7
Average value	54639	76913	86704	106963	134739	174138	165539	197845	226357.4	247443.7

Table 4. Amount of investments in fixed assets per capita in the first group's regions (rubles)

	2003	2004	2005	2006	2007	2008	2009	2010	2011	2012	2013
Belgorod Region	10140	15000	23167	34419	55045	68421	47826	62865	82123	88527	83717
Voronezh Region	8357	9321	12126	16488	27806	40213	40561	53890	66539	77218	93050
Kursk Region	8269	12594	15054	19871	28981	40739	36152	40779	52083	56188	63213
Lipetsk Region	14262	22231	25339	37382	54442	74378	71484	86502	96265	79034	87033
Smolensk Region	10997	11032	13968	15689	24844	37380	34742	49429	57933	57648	57505
Tver Region	15189	20766	16746	17288	26121	36361	51115	60851	70034	60029	60560
Average value	10257	14786	18921	27040	41568	55938	49006	61009	74252	75242	74180

As for Smolensk and Tver Regions, here, just as in the case of the two leading regions, the situation was found to be quite predictable. Inherently having the minimum opportunities not only for efficient development of their economies but simply for maintaining them at a level comparable to those of their powerful group-mates, these regions obviously have not coped with this difficult task. If Smolensk Region could not take full advantage of the benefits of its geographic position, the situation with Tver region is much more difficult. In the latter's case, the geographic location between the two largest "metropolitan" agglomerations of the country, which initially seemed to be beneficial, actually backfired in the region. The influence of the Moscow agglomeration, to a greater extent, and of St. Petersburg, to a much lesser extent, which has highly disproportionally increased during the recent years, as well as hyper outgrowth of Moscow Region (stimulated by administrative and political measures rather than by natural economic growth factors) had a negative effect on the set of socioeconomic development factors of Tver Region. Inherently featuring a serious "imperfection" in the form of extremely disproportionate settlement structure, a hyper-concentration (one rural inhabited locality per 8.84 km^2, in the context of the largest territory among regions of the Central Federal District) of rural settlements and small towns, the Region, experiencing strong migration "pull" from Moscow and St. Petersburg, could not retain the frame of its settlements network. Numerous towns and townships have not proved able, and conceptually were unable (due to proximity of the capital city), to act as "reference points" in conditions of increase of the rate of social space shrinkage. Figuratively speaking, Tver Region became similar to a multi-story house whose dwellers periodically renovate their apartments and entrances but, at the same time, can do nothing with the building foundation gradually breaking down.

Study of the dynamics of basic economic development indicators in the second group's regions (see Tables 5, 6) allows us to draw the following conclusions. During almost the entire period under consideration, the leader in terms of both gross regional product and attracted investments was Kaluga Region, featuring a combination of economic development factors that seemed to foreign investors to be optimal for the deployment of a powerful automotive cluster (plants of three automotive groups: Volvo Trucks, Peugeot–Citroen–Mitsubishi, and Volkswagen) in its territory.

Table 5. Gross regional product per capita in the second group's regions (thousand rubles)

	2003	2004	2005	2006	2007	2008	2009	2010	2011	2012
Bryansk Region	31942.3	37673.4	49923.4	62187.8	78518.8	96885.4	98014.5	114777.6	137187.1	166654
Kaluga Region	47201.9	56570.2	69192.2	84317.4	109790.3	147929.5	152611.6	186347.8	232722	286496.7
Kostroma Region	40674.0	52367.9	63304.4	78226.9	95687.2	119071.5	116856.2	146536.9	175626.6	199326.8
Oryol Region	49254.6	54411.7	64180.4	79341.5	95387.1	120531.4	113848.8	134533.8	167464.9	187706.4
Ryazan Region	49023.1	58259.1	70665.8	89010.9	102982.5	128211.5	131891.2	154844.8	186187.2	215619.2
Tambov Region	40183.2	49290.8	55573.9	70416.2	94532.5	108653.3	123512.0	131456.7	159543	188358.6
Average value	43046	51429	62140	77250	96150	120214	122789	144750	153590.6	207360.3

As expected, Bryansk Region, which inherently had little chance of winning in the economic "competition," failed to implement even its small opportunities: during the entirety of the studied period, it ranked in last place by both economic development indicators, and only in 2009 did it rank fifth by the amount of the investments attracted.

Table 6. Amount of investments in fixed assets per capita in the second group's regions (rubles)

	2003	2004	2005	2006	2007	2008	2009	2010	2011	2012	2013
Bryansk Region	4771	4987	6360	9439	16062	19478	20814	32780	37810	36974	48711
Kaluga Region	9048	10222	13286	17908	34361	65184	59440	73599	76686	95312	89396
Kostroma Region	8021	17323	19951	17014	20271	24754	16782	22549	26575	32059	33832
Oryol Region	6966	9232	11597	15568	29839	33967	24863	27175	43491	51928	56457
Ryazan Region	7825	15253	19788	21891	28550	45453	32653	35115	46223	58179	62008
Tambov Region	7078	9825	12840	17362	27512	38396	44209	49312	62886	76839	91452
Average value	7285	11140	13970	16530	26099	37872	33127	40088	48945	58548	63643

An unfavorable forecast made for Oryol Region also proved reasonable: its economy demonstrated the greatest decline among the whole group; in terms of GRP, the region fell from the first place in 2003 to the fifth in 2012.

Even the positive shift of this region by one place (from the fifth to the fourth) in the ranking of attracted investments did not help to reduce the rate of decline in regional production.

On the contrary, the situation of the regions least provided with basic socioeconomic development factors – Kostroma Region and (to a much lesser extent) Tambov Region – was found to be much more positive than that of Bryansk and Oryol Regions. Thus, Kostroma region managed to retain the fourth place by GRP in spite of the drop in investments (by this indicator, the region fell from the second to the sixth place). As for Tambov region, it not only significantly increased the rate of growth of its economy (having moved from the fifth place to the third by GRP) but also became the leader in terms of investment attraction (having risen from the fourth place to the first). Well-developed agricultural production and industry focused on processing of agricultural raw materials, as expected, became more attractive to investors than the machine-building industry dominating in the regions of this group.

Focusing on development of agriculture enabled this region to not only avoid being affected by the economic crisis that peaked in 2009 but also to increase its GRP by 12% compared to 2008. Initially standing somewhat apart, Ryazan Region, with its basic economic development factors pattern not allowing unambiguous prediction of the vector of this development, demonstrated the ability to make full use of the few advantages available to it. The region's economy succeeded in retaining the second largest GRP against the background of the actively growing economy of Kaluga Region; in addition, the region managed to maintain also its third place in the ranking of attracted investments. We now consider the dynamics of indicators characterizing the demographic situation and state of the population's health in the first group's regions (rate of natural increase of population, life expectancy indicator, and infant mortality rate) in 2003 and 2013 (see Table 7).

The pattern for all the three indicators is, in general, similar, and gives no grounds for ambiguity of interpretation: over the studied period, the places of both leading and outsider regions were stable (see Table 8). Thus, the most favorable situation in the sphere under consideration has developed in Belgorod Region: over the entire studied period, the region was distinguished by the lowest rate of population decrease and the highest life expectancy, whereas in terms of infant mortality rate in 2013, it rose from the third to the first place.

Table 7. Indicators characterizing the demographic situation and the state of the population's health in the first group's regions

	Rate of natural increase of population			Life expectancy		Infant mortality rate	
	2003	2013	Share of population above working age (%)	2003	2013	2003	2013
Belgorod Region	-7.6	-2.2	25.5	67.53	72.16	12	6.5
Voronezh Region	-10.8	-4.8	27.3	66.07	70.89	10.8	7.4
Kursk Region	-10.4	-4.5	26.9	65.34	69.66	15.8	8.3
Lipetsk Region	-8.8	-3.9	26.3	66.34	70.14	10.3	7.7
Smolensk Region	-12.9	-5.8	26.3	61.96	68.9	14	8.9
Tver Region	-14.6	-6.7	27.7	61.52	68.13	14.7	9.9
Group average	-10.85	-4.65	26.7	64.79	69.98	12.93	8.1

The following are Lipetsk and Voronezh Regions: the sum of places of both regions by the three indicators in 2013 is equal to eight. In the former region in 2003, this value was equal to five: Lipetsk Region consistently ranked second in terms of rate of natural decrease of population. However, in terms of life expectancy, it moved from the second to the third place, and by the level of infant mortality, it "drifted back" from the first place to the third. Voronezh Region, on the contrary, rose by one place in the rankings (the sum of places in 2003 is nine) on account of an increase in life expectancy. The third place is taken by Kursk Region (the sum of places in 2003 is thirteen, and in 2013 it is eleven). This region strongly reduced the infant mortality rate (by 47.5%), rising from sixth place to fourth in terms of this indicator.

The regions with the least favorable situation in the sphere of demography and the population's health in this group are Smolensk and Tver Regions, stable at fifth and sixth places, respectively, in terms of natural decrease of population and life expectancy. The growth of the latter indicator, though the group's highest in these regions (+6.94 years in Smolensk Region, and +6.61 years in Tver Region), was so low in 2003 in both regions (the lowest among all the regions of the Central Federal District) that even in 2013, these areas did not manage to catch up with their group-mates. As for the infant mortality rate, Smolensk Region fell from fourth to fifth place and Tver Region from fifth to sixth. It should be noted that the indicator of rate of natural decrease of population in 2013 in the first group of regions correlates with the share of population above working age: in Tver Region, it is, for example, the highest, whereas in Belgorod Region, it is the lowest. An exception is Smolensk Region taking the second place in 2013 in terms of the former indicator (after Belgorod Region), whereas according to the rate of population decrease, it was ranked, as mentioned above, in next-to-last place.

Table 8. Places of the first group's regions by indicators characterizing the demographic situation and the state of the population's health

	Sum of places		Rate of natural increase of population			Life expectancy		Infant mortality rate	
	2003	2013	2003	2013	Share of population above working age	2003	2013	2003	2013
Belgorod Region	5	3	1	1	1	1	1	3	1
Voronezh Region	9	8	4	4	4	3	2	2	2
Kursk Region	13	11	3	3	3	4	4	6	4
Lipetsk Region	5	8	2	2	2	2	3	1	3
Smolensk Region	14	15	5	5	2	5	5	4	5
Tver Region	17	18	6	6	5	6	6	5	6

Just as for the first group's regions, the regions of the second group featured, over the period under study, a negative natural increase of population. The rates of population decrease recorded by statistics correspond, as a whole, to the existing age structure of the population: the regions with low population increase rates usually have a high share of unemployable people (Ryazan and Tambov Regions), whereas the regions with "young" population structure are characterized also by lower rates of population decrease (Kaluga and Kostroma Regions) (see Table 9).

Alongside this, Bryansk Region, which had the lowest share of unemployable population in 2012, was only in the third place in terms of natural increase of population (see Table 10). On the contrary, Ryazan Region, in the last place by the unemployable population share, rose from sixth place in 2003 to fourth in 2013 in terms of population decrease.

Table 9. Indicators characterizing the demographic situation and the state of the population's health in the second group's regions

	Rate of natural increase of population			Life expectancy		Infant mortality rate	
	2003	2013	Share of population above working age (%)	2003	2013	2003	2013
Bryansk Region	-10.4	-4.8	25.8	64.07	69.75	14.3	8.9
Kaluga Region	-10.2	-3.5	26.4	64.26	70.02	13.6	9.4
Kostroma Region	-11.3	-3.4	26.0	62.88	69.86	14.2	8.6
Oryol Region	-9.8	-5.2	27.1	65.5	70.22	10.7	8.6
Ryazan Region	-12.6	-5.0	28.5	64.21	70.74	12.9	9.1
Tambov Region	-11.2	-6.6	28.1	65.34	70.93	11.7	5.5
Group average	-10.9	-4.75	26.98	64.4	70.25	12.9	8.35

With respect to the life expectancy indicator in 2013, the leader is Tambov Region, which was in the second place in 2003; in return, the second place was taken by Ryazan Region, which was fourth in 2003. As for the third place, it was taken by Oryol Region, which fell after being first in 2003. Kostroma Region also improved this factor, while Bryansk and Kaluga Regions showed decline in this factor.

Table 10. Places of the second group's regions by indicators characterizing the demographic situation and the state of the population's health

	Rate of natural increase of population			Life expectancy		Infant mortality rate	
	2003	2013	Share of population above working age	2003	2013	2003	2013
Bryansk Region	3	3	1	5	6	6	3
Kaluga Region	2	2	3	3	4	4	5
Kostroma Region	5	1	2	6	5	5	2
Oryol Region	1	5	4	1	3	1	2
Ryazan Region	6	4	6	4	2	3	4
Tambov Region	4	6	5	2	1	2	1

In terms of the dynamics of infant mortality rate in the regions under study in 2003 and 2013, Kostroma and Bryansk Regions stand out against other regions – both shifted up by as much as three steps, achieving third and second place, respectively. Tambov Region rose to first place from second. Kaluga,

Oryol, and Ryazan Regions, on the contrary, somewhat worsened their positions, having descended by a step.

Finally, we analyze the dynamics of the data characterizing the population's educational level in the regions of both groups over the period from 2002 to 2010 (see Table 11). It should be noted that all the above regions gradually increased the educational potential of their population. A stable leader in this sphere, over the period under study, was Voronezh Region, which has one of the most developed systems of higher and postgraduate education in the country as a whole. The second and the third places, at the start of the period, were taken by Tver and Belgorod Regions, respectively. Next, with a slight gap between each other, were Smolensk and Kursk Regions. The last place, in terms of two of the three studied indicators, was taken by Lipetsk Region.

Table 11. Places of the first group's regions by indicators characterizing the quality of the population in 2002

	Sum of places	Share of persons with science degrees (pers.) in relation to the average annual number of people employed in the economy (thousand pers.)		Share of persons with higher education in relation to the average annual number of people employed in the economy (pers.)		Share of persons with post-graduate education in relation to the average annual number of people employed in the economy (pers.)	
		2002	Place	2002	Place	2002	Place
The Belgorod Region	10	0.197	3	0.191	2	0.00227	5
The Voronezh Region	4	0.599	2	0.201	1	0.00353	1
The Kursk Region	13	0.187	4	0.167	6	0.00261	3
The Lipetsk Region	16	0.044	6	0.180	4	0.00203	6
The Smolensk Region	12	0.106	5	0.184	3	0.00241	4
The Tver Region	8	0.747	1	0.176	5	0.00299	2
Group average		0.313		0.183		0.00264	

In 2010, the situation in the sphere of higher education significantly changed throughout all regions of the first group (except, as already mentioned, Voronezh Region). Thus, Belgorod Region rose to second place, having considerably increased the share of persons with postgraduate education (Belgorod State University became the only higher education institution in the Central Federal District, besides the capital city's universities, that was awarded the status of "the National Research University" in 2010) (see Table 12).

Table 12. Places of the first group's regions by indicators characterizing the quality of the population in 2010

	Sum of places	Share of persons with science degrees (pers.) in relation to the average annual number of people employed in the economy (thousand pers.)		Share of persons with higher education in relation to the average annual number of people employed in the economy (pers.)		Share of persons with post-graduate education in relation to the average annual number of people employed in the economy (pers.)	
		2010	Place	2010	Place	2010	Place
Belgorod Region	6	0.445	3	0.387	2	0.0118	1
Voronezh Region	4	0.872	1	0.397	1	0.0097	2
Kursk Region	15	0.251	4	0.319	6	0.0085	5
Lipetsk Region	11	0.183	5	0.358	3	0.0093	3
Smolensk Region	17	0.129	6	0.323	5	0.0080	6
Tver Region	10	0.785	2	0.332	4	0.0091	4
Group average		0.444		0.353		0.00948	

Tver Region, on the contrary, lowered its rank to the third, almost without increasing the share of people with science degrees in the structure of its employable population, and it was significantly inferior to several regions in terms of the number of persons with postgraduate education. The fourth place was rapidly taken by Lipetsk Region, which increased its rates by all the three indicators. Kursk Region remained in the fifth place; Smolensk Region was in the last place, and its ranks fell in terms of the three indicators.

The "top performers" among the second group's regions in terms of the population's educational level in 2002 were Kaluga and Oryol Regions, the former taking the leading place in the share of persons with higher education and the share of scientists in the structure of the economically active population (see Table 13).

Table 13. Places of the second group's regions by indicators characterizing the quality of the population in 2002

	Sum of places	Share of persons with science degrees (pers.) in relation to the average annual number of people employed in the economy (thousand pers.)		Share of persons with higher education in relation to the average annual number of people employed in the economy (pers.)		Share of persons with post-graduate education in relation to the average annual number of people employed in the economy (pers.)	
		2002	Place	2002	Place	2002	Place
Bryansk Region	17	0.0798	6	0.169	5	0.00190	6
Kaluga Region	4	2.272	1	0.219	1	0.00326	2
Kostroma Region	14	0.094	5	0.184	4	0.00219	5
Oryol Region	6	0.356	2	0.185	3	0.00337	1
Ryazan Region	10	0.254	4	0.190	2	0.00251	4
Tambov Region	12	0.326	3	0.168	6	0.00253	3
Group average		0.537		0.188		0.00284	

The third place was taken by Ryazan Region, whereas the last ranks were taken by Tambov, Kostroma, and Bryansk Regions. In 2010, Oryol Region took first place, and Kaluga and Ryazan Regions "settled down" in the second place (see Table 14). Although the former lost its positions in terms of the two indicators (having shifted down from second place to sixth according to the share of persons with postgraduate education), the latter maximized its rank in the share of persons with higher education in the population structure. The third place was shared by Bryansk and Tambov Regions. The former greatly raised the share of persons with postgraduate education, however, having increased the share of people with science degrees very slightly. Most probably, this region's rank was possibly due to its 2002 highest share of people under working age among the second group of regions (i.e., potential enrollees) and the availability of a wide network of branches of the capital city's universities in the region at that time. Tambov Region mended its situation on account of a slight improvement in its ranking in two positions and retained its place in the share of scientists in the economically active population structure. The last, fourth place, was taken by Kostroma Region, which lowered its ranks on two of the three indicators.

We consider the change in criminality indicators over 2003-2013 in six regions of the first group (see Table 15). The average criminality level in the first group's regions over the period under study amounted to 1,805.7 recorded crimes per 100 thousand pers. Increase in the average criminality level over the period from 2003 to 2006/2007 throughout the regions was 36.5%; the decline in this indicator over the period from 2007/2008 to 2012/2013 was equal to 43.7%; and the general decline in criminality level from 2003 to 2012/2013 amounted to 23.4% (see Table 16). Alongside this, the studied group of regions was distinguished by considerable non-uniformity and fundamental differences both in criminality level and the dynamics of this indicator in individual regions over the period under consideration (see Diagram 1).

Table 14. Places of the second group's regions by indicators characterizing the quality of the population in 2010

	Sum of places	Share of persons with science degrees (pers.) in relation to the average annual number of people employed in the economy (thousand pers.)		Share of persons with higher education in relation to the average annual number of people employed in the economy (pers.)		Share of persons with post-graduate education in relation to the average annual number of people employed in the economy (pers.)	
		2010	Place	2010	Place	2010	Place
Bryansk Region	10	0.087	5	0.34	4	0.010	1
Kaluga Region	9	1.957	1	0.345	2	0.00757	6
Kostroma Region	17	0.065	6	0.293	6	0.00769	5
Oryol Region	8	0.436	2	0.343	3	0.00861	3
Ryazan Region	9	0.346	4	0.354	1	0.00799	4
Tambov Region	10	0.355	3	0.314	5	0.00945	2
Group average		0.578		0.326		0.0085	

Table 15. Criminality level in the first group's regions over 2003-2013

	2003	2004	2005	2006	2007	2008	2009	2010	2011	2012	2013	Average
Belgorod Region	1264	1280	1670	1594	1397	1257	1308	1099	1036	968	968	1258
Voronezh Region	1267	1162	1568	1662	1709	1684	1535	1385	1315	1158	1306	1432
Kursk Region	1658	1804	2199	2662	2453	1955	1778	1623	1504	1347	1180	1833
Lipetsk Region	1631	1608	1886	1777	1763	1526	1378	1174	1158	1188	1143	1475
Smolensk Region	2077	2334	2824	2798	2484	2358	2354	2116	1856	1737	1519	2223
Tver Region	1970	2045	2866	2982	2811	2597	2483	2204	2150	1905	1515	2321
Average criminality level in group	1644.5	1705.5	2168.8	2245.8	2102.8	1896.2	1806	1600.2	1503.2	1383.8	1272	1757

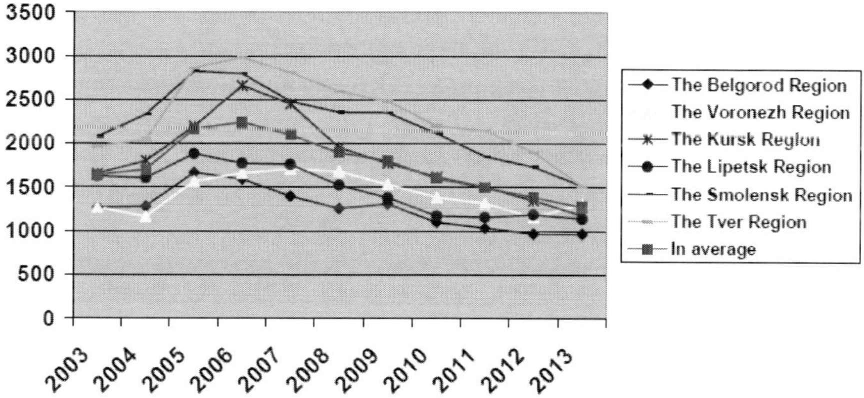

Diagram 1. Dynamics of criminality level in the first group's regions over 2003-2013.

The minimum criminality level (the average both over the analyzed period and over given years) was observable in the statistics in Belgorod Region: here, this figure was the smallest over almost the entire period (with the exception of 2004-2005) and averaged 1,258 crimes per 100 thousand pers. Next were Voronezh and Lipetsk Regions with an average level of criminality over the analyzed period equal to 1,432 and 1,475 crimes, respectively. Lipetsk Region had the minimum growth in criminality level over 2004-2005 among the regions of the group under study, was equal only to 15.6%, whereas its decline in criminality level over 2005-2012 was, on the contrary, the highest and amounted to 29.9%. However, over the period from 2010 to 2013, criminality in the region actually remained at the same level.

Kursk Region again appears to be an "average performer" among the first group's regions, in terms of criminality. An average criminality level in this region amounted, over the period under study, to 1,833 crimes per 100 thousand pers., i.e., it did not exceed by much the average value for the group as a whole. Over the period from 2003 to 2008, the criminality level in Kursk Region exceeded the average criminality level in this group's regions, and over 2009-2012, the value of this indicator in Kursk Region and its dynamics actually matched the level and dynamics of the average criminality level in the regions of the first group.

The end of the criminality rating list for the first group's regions is occupied by Smolensk and Tver Regions: their average criminality level over the period under review amounted to 2,223 and 2,321 crimes per 100 thousand pers., respectively. These regions were the "leaders" in criminality level both in 2003 and 2013. The latter region was also distinguished by one of the highest increments of this indicator: over 2003-2006, it rose by 51.4%. Next, we consider the trends in variation in criminality indicators in the second group's regions. The common trend in criminality level variation in the Central Federal District regions included in this group coincides, in general, with the situation in the first group's regions and in Russia as a whole (see Table 17 and Diagram 2).

Table 16. Dynamics of criminality level in the first group's regions by periods (%)

	Increase in criminality level over 2003-2003-2005/2007	Decline in criminality level over 2006/2008-2012/2013	Decline in criminality level over 2003-2012/ 2013
Belgorod Region	+32.1	-42	-23.4
Voronezh Region	+34.9	-32.2	-8.6
Kursk Region	+60.5	-55.7	-28.8
Lipetsk Region	+15.6	-37	-29.9
Smolensk Region	+35.9	-46.2	-26.8
Tver Region	+51.4	-49.2	-23.1
Group average	+36.5	-43.7	-23.4

Table 17. Criminality level in the second group's regions over 2003-2013

	2003	2004	2005	2006	2007	2008	2009	2010	2011	2012	2013	Average
Bryansk Region	1808	1854	2316	2184	2140	2041	1973	1833	1533	1488	1527	1881,5
Kaluga Region	1769	2035	2560	2567	2289	2121	1963	1776	1496	1468	1565	1964,5
Kostroma Region	2193	2202	2440	2309	1969	1606	1553	1482	1394	1265	1164	1779,7
Oryol Region	1897	1929	2256	2471	2430	2061	1853	1732	1610	1699	1580	1956,2
Ryazan Region	1024	965	1457	1382	1184	1165	959	916	845	832	849	1052,5
Tambov Region	1328	1400	2014	2063	1828	1600	1467	1259	1247	1087	1093	1489,6
Average criminality level in group	1769.8	1862.6	2257.5	2234.1	2035.1	1792.8	1672	1523.8	1381.5	1314.1	1296.3	1687.3

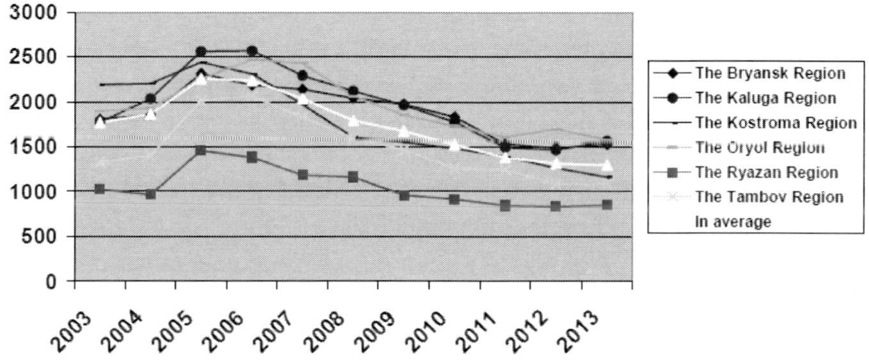

Diagram 2. Dynamics of criminality level in the second group's regions over 2003-2013.

The criminality level increased with various rates over the period from 2003 to 2006 and declined, also with varying rate, over 2007-2012 (see Table 18). In 2013, the statistics once more recorded an increase in criminality level in four regions. The average level of criminality in the second group's regions over the period under study amounted to 1,687.3 crimes per 100 thousand pers. i.e., it was slightly lower than that of the first group. The increase in criminality level in the regions over the period from 2003 to 2005/2006 amounted on average to 27.6%, whereas the decline of this indicator over the period from 2006/2007 to 2012-2013 was equal to 42.8%; the general decline in criminality level from 2003 to 2012-2013 amounted to 22.5%. Alongside this, the studied group of regions is distinguished by even greater non-uniformity than the first group of regions, both in terms of criminality level and in the dynamics of this indicator in the individual regions over the reviewed period.

The lowest criminality level (both the average over the analyzed period and over the given years) was recorded by the statistics in the Ryazan Region: in this area, this indicator had the minimum value over the entire period under review and averaged 1,052.5 crimes per 100 thousand pers. In 2013, for the first time since 2005, a slight increase in the criminality level was observed in the region. The second place is taken by Tambov Region, with an average criminality level equal to 1489.6 crimes per 100 thousand pers. In 2013, a slight increase in the value of this indicator (+ 0.5%) was also recorded in Tambov Region. The average criminality level over the reviewed period in other regions of the second group was significantly higher than in the above two regions: it ranged from 1,779.7 in Kostroma Region to 1,964.5 in Kaluga

Region. The average annual increase rate of this indicator in these regions was less than the average annual increase rate of criminality level over the entire group, whereas at a rate exceeding the average for the group, the criminality level declined only in Kaluga and Kostroma Regions.

Table 18. Rates of variation in criminality level in the second group's regions over 2004-2013 (%)

	2004	2005	2006	2007	2008	2009	2010	2011	2012	2013	Average annual rate of criminality level increase over 2004-2007	Average annual rate of criminality level decline over 2006-2012/2013
Bryansk Region	+2.5	+24.9	-5.7	-2	-4.6	-3.3	-7.1	-16.4	-2.9	+2.6	+13.7	-6
Kaluga Region	+15	+25.8	+0.3	-10.8	-7.3	-7.4	-9.5	-15.8	-1.9	+6.6	+13.7	-8.9
Kostroma Region	+0.4	+10.8	-5.4	-14.7	-18.4	-3.3	-4.6	-5.3	-9.2	-8	+5.6	-8.6
Oryol Region	+1.7	+16.9	+9.5	-1.7	-15.2	-10.1	-6.5	-7	+5.5	-7	+9.4	-7.9
Ryazan Region	-5.8	+51	-5.1	-14.3	-1.6	-17.7	-4.5	-7.7	-1.5	+2	+51	-7.5
Tambov Region	+5.4	+43.8	+2.4	-11.4	-12.5	-8.3	-14.2	-0.9	-12.8	+0.5	+17.2	-10
Average rate of criminality level increase/decline	+5.2	+21.2	-1	-8.9	-11.9	-6.7	-8.9	-9.3	-4.9	-0.5	+15.2	-8.15

The latter region was also characterized by the highest dynamics of decline in criminality level, both over 2006-2013 and over 2003 to 2013: –52.3% and –46.9%, respectively (see Table 19). As a result, according to criminality level, Kostroma Region rose from sixth place in 2003 to third in 2013; Bryansk Region remained in fourth place; Kaluga and Oryol Regions, on the contrary, shifted down: Kaluga Region by two places and Oryol Region by one place (see Table 20). In the latter region, the average criminality level over the period from 2003 to 2013, officially, was not the highest (1,956.2); however, over 2007-2012/2013, this region was characterized by one of the least significant (–36%) values of criminality level decline, and, in addition, this decline was the lowest over the entire period under study (–16.7%).

We now juxtapose the obtained data on the dynamics of economic and social development of the regions of both groups with the identified trends and patterns of criminality therein.

Table 19. Dynamics of criminality level in the second group's regions by periods (%)

	Increase in criminality level over 2003-2005/2006 (%)	Decline in criminality level over 2006/2007-2012/2013 (%)	Decline in criminality level over 2003-2012/2013 (%)
Bryansk Region	+28.1	-35.7	-17.7
Kaluga Region	+45.1	-42.8	-17
Kostroma Region	+11.3	-52.3	-46.9
Oryol Region	+30.3	-36	-16.7
Ryazan Region	+42.3	-42.9	-18.7
Tambov Region	+55.3	-47.3	-18.1
In average in the group	+27.6	-42.8	-22.5

Table 20. Places of the second group's regions by criminality level in 2003 and 2013

	2003	2013
Bryansk Region	4	4
Kaluga Region	3	5
Kostroma Region	6	3
Oryol Region	5	6
Ryazan Region	1	1
Tambov Region	2	2

An obvious "favorite" of the first group in all respects, is, of course, Belgorod Region, with its advanced, diversified, and rapidly progressing economy. Apparently, due to the influence of positive trends in the economic sphere of the region's life, its social "properties" have also greatly improved: the region not only consistently excels in the demographic characteristics of the population but has also gradually begun to dominate in terms of the accumulated educational potential of its inhabitants. All this allowed Belgorod Region to become one of the most attractive regions in Russia (after Moscow and Moscow Region, as well as St. Petersburg), a true "growth point." This, in our opinion, explains well also its most positive situation among the regions of both groups in terms of criminality.

Voronezh Region, which, as already mentioned, inherently was seriously inferior to Lipetsk Region in terms of economic potential, has been able to make more efficient use of its own (roughly comparable to Lipetsk Region) basic advantages of socioeconomic development and to demonstrate the constant growth both of its economy and the social characteristics of the population. As a result, the criminality indicators, which at the beginning of the studied period were worse than those of Lipetsk Region, significantly improved by 2012. As for Lipetsk Region, it is quite possible that although some of the difficulties identified in the development of the region's economic base made it impossible to enhance the social well-being of its population in all spheres, nevertheless, certain progress in this region was evident. However, the contradictions related to the development of the economy and the social sphere did not permit lowering of the criminality level in this region to the highest possible extent. This conclusion is also confirmed by the actual stabilization of the criminality level in Lipetsk Region over 2010-2012, whereas in other regions of the group, this indicator gradually declined during this period.

The inherently low coverage of Kursk Region with basic socioeconomic development factors did not allow the region to reach the advanced positions in terms of both economic sphere development and social capital accumulation. However, neither the region's economy nor its social sphere have degraded, which, apparently, allowed it to maintain criminality "within normal limits" in the region.

Unfortunately, the same cannot be said about Smolensk and Tver Regions. Being obvious outsiders from the viewpoint of both economic development and improvement of the population's social well-being, these regions were naturally distinguished, in the course of the reviewed period, also by the worst situation in the criminality sphere. Alongside this, it is fair to say that while the causes of deterioration of the overall socioeconomic situation in Smolensk Region seem to be brought about by the ineffectiveness of the region's administration policy in these areas of the region's life, the causes of a similar situation in Tver Region, in our opinion, were, figuratively speaking, of "genetic" character. Evident disproportions in the established settlement system (which is, in fact, the skeleton of the "body" of the regional socioeconomic system), under existing circumstances of "super-influence" and attraction exerted by Moscow and Moscow Region, eventually led to the fracture of this support frame of the region's socioeconomic sphere. Therefore, despite some progress in the development of the region's economic base (for example, an increase in investment attractiveness of the region in 2009-2012), these disproportions made it impossible to achieve improvement in the characteristics of the population's social well-being.

Further, we proceed to the regions of the second group. It should be remembered that in Kaluga Region, the highest average criminality level was recorded. Simultaneously, this region has been the second group's leader in terms of economic development rate since 2007. According to conclusions made by Soviet criminologists, socioeconomic relations transformation associated with rapid economic growth almost inevitably causes an increase in criminality level. Kaluga Region was no exception: the criminality level featured an increased average annual rate of growth (+13.7%), and, as a result, rose by 45.1% over 2003-2006. Meanwhile, the region's economic growth has not yet led to significant changes in the social sphere: demographic indicators have deteriorated, and the region's superiority in terms of the population's educational potential has been lost. Nevertheless, the criminality level in the region declined at increased annual average rates, but in 2011-2012, it stabilized and increased again in 2013. What its future vector will be, depends, in our opinion, largely on the region's administration or, rather, on its capability to competently and foresightedly take advantage of the progress achieved in the economy in the course of reforming the region's social sphere.

Almost equal to the average criminality level in Kaluga Region was that of Oryol Region (1,956.2 crimes per 100 thousand pers.). It would be no mistake to classify this region as the main "loser" of all the regions of the second group: its economy and social sphere have undergone the greatest degradation over the period under review. It should be remembered that only in terms of the indicators characterizing the population's educational level did Oryol Region manage to maintain and even slightly improve its rating in the group. As a result of such development of the socioeconomic situation, the criminality level growth rate in the region increased, whereas the rate of its decline was low. The decline in criminality level over the entire reviewed period was also found to be minimal: only by 16.7%, with an average of 22.5%. As a result, this region moved from fifth place in criminality level in 2003 to sixth in 2013.

A similar pattern, but with a slightly more favorable "shade," showed up in Bryansk Region (with the average criminality level of 1,881.5 crimes per 100 thousand pers). The stable fifth or sixth place of this region in terms of economic growth level, was, naturally, not able to provide implementation of a large-scale task of its human capital quality improvement; however, the region has somewhat succeeded in reducing infant mortality and in improving the situation also on several indicators characterizing the population's educational level. Perhaps these and other minor successes in Bryansk Region allowed the prevention of such serious deterioration of the criminality situation as in the Oryol Region.

Proceeding to Kostroma Region, we would like to recall that this region was originally characterized by us as a territory that had (based on its coverage with basic socioeconomic development factors) the least chances of achieving positive results in improvement of its population's social well-being. Nonetheless, the region succeeded in relation to several other indicators. Thus, it did not slow down the rate of its economic development even against the background of the rapidly growing economies of some of its group-mates; there was improvement in all indicators in the demographic sphere, and only the educational level of the region's population – it should be remembered – changed in the opposite direction. Most likely, this all contributed to considerable improvement of the situation in criminality in the region: let us recall that in terms of criminality level, Kostroma Region moved from sixth place in 2003 to third in 2013.

Considering Tambov Region, it may safely be concluded that only the absence of export-oriented economic sectors and urban agglomerations prevented this region from developing its social sphere to the level of Belgorod Region and, consequently, to slow down the criminality growth rate over 2003-2006. However, the region's economy based on agricultural production showed significant progress over the period under review; thanks largely to this progress, as well as to the existing structure of settlement and industrial facilities location, the human capital characteristics in Tambov Region also improved.

This result, in turn, smoothed also the region's criminality situation, which currently is, as noted above, one of the most favorable throughout the Central Federal District.

Ryazan Region was distinguished by the lowest average criminality level over the period under review, though it should be remembered that this region did not have any pronounced advantages or obvious disadvantages from the viewpoint of prospects for its further socioeconomic development; thus, the "compass needle" of such development might well swing to either one or the other side. Time has shown that the region is steadily moving in the right direction: its economy is developing at sufficiently rapid rates, the situation in the demographic sphere has improved by most of the indicators, and all the characteristics of the population's educational level have also tangibly increased. Hence, the most favorable position of Ryazan Region in terms of criminality level is quite explainable.

Therefore, the results of analysis of socioeconomic processes development features versus the criminality trends identified in the above regions suggest the existence of the following patterns:

1. among the abovementioned regions, over the period from 2003 to 2013, the regions with the nature and vector of socioeconomic development that most comply with a positive socioeconomic processes development model at the level of region-scale social systems (Belgorod, Voronezh, Ryazan, and Tambov Regions) were distinguished by the highest value and (or) positive dynamics of indicators characterizing the results of life activity of the population of these territories in the socioeconomic aspects and of indicators reflecting the quality of the population itself. As a result of studying the criminality trends, it was found that the same group of regions had also been characterized, over the mentioned period, by a more favorable situation in criminogenic terms. On the contrary, in the regions where a negative scenario of socioeconomic processes development has materialized, the most unfavorable situation in terms of criminality has also developed (Smolensk, Tver, and Oryol Regions). The lack of distinctness of the general vector of development of these processes in Bryansk, Kaluga, Kostroma, Kursk, and Lipetsk Regions seems to have caused uncertainty of interpretation of the current criminogenic situation in these areas;
2. the degree of social welfare of the region's population is largely associated with the level and dynamics of its economic base development; alongside this, the deterioration in the condition of the region's settlement structure and existence of distinct tendencies of its social space shrinkage are the main disruptive factors in its development as a whole. This is clearly evident in the analysis of criminality in the regions in which the network settlement underwent the greatest deformation over the period under review (2003-2010), namely, in Tver Region, where the highest average criminality level was recorded;
3. high growth rates of a region's economy without changes in the area of the population's life quality assurance also do not contribute to radical improvement of the situation in the criminality sphere (the Kaluga Region); maintaining a certain balance between conditions of the economic and social spheres in the region can prevent a surge of

criminal activeness of its population (the Bryansk, Kursk, and Kostroma Regions);

4. in those cases where this cannot be done, when the stagnated economy is not capable of keeping the region's social sphere "afloat," criminality indicators also seriously deteriorate (Oryol, Smolensk Regions), although not to such an extent as in the regions with a strongly pronounced tendency of social space shrinkage.

CONCLUSION

The main pattern that manifested itself as a result of comparing the region's initial "chances" of success in its socioeconomic base development (from the viewpoint of the identified patterns of spatial development of socioeconomic processes) with the actual results achieved on this way and with the criminality rates officially recorded by statistics consists of the following. The social well-being of the region's population (with criminality level being one of the main indicators of its state) depends, first, on the potential possessed by each of the regional socioeconomic systems in terms of the theory of center-periphery relations, and, second, on the degree of implementation of this potential defined by actual results achieved in economic, demographic, social, and other aspects of development of the regional systems. The higher this potential and the wider the range of opportunities for successful socioeconomic development of a region, the better the results it will achieve in this respect. Inadequate implementation of the enshrined potential leads to the deterioration of the population's social well-being and, inevitably, to an increase in negative trends in the criminality sphere.

These results suggest that in conditions of not only the centrally planned but also the market method of economic activity, a hypothesis, based on empirical data, that considers deterioration of criminality indicators as a sign of manifestation of social and economic ill-being in a certain territorial social system is confirmed. This means once again that (but, hopefully, at a qualitatively different level) a long-standing idea stating that the root of criminality lies in negative changes in the socioeconomic sphere of society is proven. However, under current conditions, knowing general patterns of evolution of this sphere, we can both determine the nature and estimate the extent of such negative trends, and therefore (having an idea about the nature of relationships between changes in the socioeconomic sphere and in the sphere of criminality), we are able to make relatively exact predictions of changes in indicators of criminality itself. As a result, a seemingly important step is taken to achieve the main goal of criminological science, namely, to comprehend the principles of functioning of criminality as a social phenomenon and to develop a mechanism for influencing it, i.e., to obtain, in the foreseeable future, the possibility of implementation of full-scale social control over criminality.

In general, the results of the study eloquently state that in the context of understanding of criminality as an inherent property of society, and of its indicators – as characteristics of the state of the social organism, a need has arisen for turning away from the established paradigm of searching for causes of criminality as a goal of criminological research. Spatial analysis of criminality acts as a means of diagnosing the presence or absence of deviations of positive or negative nature in socioeconomic development of territorial social systems. Therefore, criminological studies focusing on similar subjects should be a part of large-scale and complex investigations on the problems of stable socioeconomic development of society.

REFERENCES

[1] Babaev, M., Karpets, I., Kuznetsova, E., Nikiforov, A., et al. (1971). *The study of crime in urban and rural*. Moscow: Legal literature.

[2] Babaev, M., Kuznetsova, E., Urlanis, E. (1976). *The impact of demographic processes on crime*. Moscow: Legal literature.

[3] Fujita, M., Krugman, P. and Venables, A. J. (2001). *The spatial economy. Sities, Regions, and International Trade*. Cambridge, MA: MIT Press.

[4] Kuznetsova, Olga, A. (2013). Pyramid of Factors of Regional Socio-Economic Development. *Question of Economics* 2:121-131.

[5] Kolomak Eugene, A. (2013). Uneven Spatial Development n Russia: Explanations of New Economic Geography. *Questions of Economics* 2: 132-149.

[6] National Census. (2002). http://perepis2002.ru/index.html?id=13.

[7] National Census. (2010). http://www.gks.ru/free_doc/new_site/perepis 2010/croc/perepis_itogi1612.htm.

[8] Erik S. Reinert (2011) *How Rich Countries Got Rich... And Why Poor Countries Stay Poor*. Moscow: State University – Higher School of Economics.

[9] Raska, E. (1987) Criminality as an Indicator of the Social Space Status (On Grounds of the Territorial Approach to Study of Criminality). In: *Theoretical Problems of Studying Territorial Differences in Criminality*. Issue 761. p. 18-29. Tartu: Tartu University Press.

[10] *Regions of Russia. Socio-economic indicators*. (2003). Moscow: Rosstat.

[11] *Regions of Russia. Socio-economic indicators*. (2011). Moscow: Rosstat.

[12] *Regions of Russia. Socio-economic indicators*. (2013). Moscow: Rosstat.

[13] Spiridonov, L., Leps, A. (1985). Theoretical Issues of Studying Territorial Differences in Criminality. In: *Theoretical Problems of Studying Territorial Differences in Criminality*. Issue 725. p. 3-18. Tartu: Tartu University Press.

[14] *The impact of social conditions on the spatial differences in crime*. (1977). Moscow: Publishing VNIISZ.

In: Advances in Criminology Research
Editor: Julia Guzman
ISBN: 978-1-63483-180-2

Chapter 2

INTEGRATED CRIMINOLOGY AND BIOLOGICAL RELATED CRIMINOLOGY FACING WHITE COLLAR CRIME

Tage Alalehto*
Department of Sociology, Umeå University, Sweden

ABSTRACT

During the last two decades the rise of integrated approaches and biosocial approaches has given criminology a fresh theoretical and empirical approach. However, a full scale integration of these two approaches has not come to a conclusion over the etiological question of what forms the criminal mind. The aim of this article is to give an argument whereby the agenda of white collar crime research can be developed by a synthesis of integrated and biosocial factors. The argument takes its standpoint in one of the recent theories on white collar crime research today, the crime-as-choice theory by Shover, Hochstetler & Alalehto (2012). The theory proposes an integrated model of factors working on different levels. For example, the linkage between lacks of credible oversight on aggregated level, the existence of a crime-facilitative culture on organizational level, and propensities towards aggressiveness, thrill-seeking, resilience, and entitlement on individual level. However, as a typical social scientific theory the crime-as-choice

* Address: Tage Alalehto; Department of Sociology, Umeå University, 901 87 Umeå, Sweden; e-mail: Tage.Alalehto@soc.umu.se; 046-090-786 54 30; 046-090-786 66 94.

theory lacks a complete etiological argument behind its proposed proximate causality. I elaborate upon the etiological concepts from the fields of evolutionary theory and institutional theory how the crime-as-choice theory can get an even more coherent structure between ultimate and proximate causes.

Keywords: Etiology, white collar crime, crime-as-choice theory

During the last two decades the rise of integrated approaches and biosocial approaches has given criminology a fresh theoretical and empirical approach. Yet a full scale integration of these two approaches has not come to a conclusion over the etiological question of what forms the criminal mind. From an integrative approach, the aim has been to combine between-group variables (e.g. correlations between sex and crime) with within-individual variables (e.g. correlations between low self-control, aggressiveness and crime) to form an explanation of crime in order to understand the particular mechanisms which operate between institutional, organizational, and individual levels (e.g. Agnew, 2004; Farrington, 2003, 2008; Laub & Sampson, 2003; Piquero, Farrington, & Blumstein, 2007; Wikström & Sampson, 2009). This approach has been criticized from a biosocial point of view, because it places too much emphasis on environmental factors. Biosocial criminologists have suggested that the explanation of crime should be complemented by the study of genes, hormones, neurons, and the evolutionary history of phenotypes in order to understand the whole variation of crime (Boisvert, Wright, Knopik, & Vaske, 2012; Ellis & Walsh, 1997; Walsh & Beaver, 2009; Walsh & Ellis, 2003; Wright & Boisvert, 2009).

Related to the white collar crime agenda, a combination of these two approaches has not yet been used in white collar crime research despite the awareness and willfulness among scholars in white collar crime research toward updating criminological theory in integrated theory (Benson & Simpson, 2009; Menard & Morris, 2012; Piquero & Benson, 2004), life course approach (Benson, 2002; Weisburd, Waring, & Chayet, 2001), and biosocial criminology (Beaver & Holtfreter, 2009; Kristy Holtfreter, Beaver, Reisig, & Pratt, 2010; Walsh & Beaver, 2009). Thereby the agenda of white collar crime has not reached any full integration with evolutionary forms of explanation (DeLisi & Piquero, 2011; Mangels, 2000).

To the casual reader, it can be appropriate to give a brief description of biologically related criminology. Biologically related criminology refers to five perspectives which is more or less intertwined to each other. They are:

behavior genetics (investigating the variation in individual behavior), molecular genetics (investigating which specific gene matters when individuals vary in their behavior), neuroscience (investigating the mental life of individuals), biology (investigating other biological parts as resting heart rate, skin conductance, etc.) and evolutionary psychology (a meta-approach to investigate the origins of human behavior) (Beaver, Barnes, & Boutwell, 2014).

In this chapter I will mainly concentrate my topic on the evolutionary psychology approach. But to some degree even incorporate concepts from behavior and molecular genetics, specifically Gene x Environment interaction (GxE). However, evolutionary psychology refers to the universal human nature consisted of domain-specific psychological mechanisms. "A psychological mechanism is an information-processing procedure or 'decision rule' which evolution by natural and sexual selection has equipped humans to possess in order to solve an adaptive problem (a problem of survival or reproduction). Unlike decision rules in decision theory or game theory, however, psychological mechanisms mostly operate behind our conscious thinking. Evolved psychological mechanisms produce preferences and values, which rational actors then pursue within their constraints, and they also engender emotions." (Kanazawa, 2003:38).

The aim of this chapter is to apply an evolutionary point of view to an existing socio-economic perspective explicitly presented by the theory of crime-as-choice. The topic is to develop an etiology for the theory of crime-as-choice by a new look at the interdisciplinary, multi-methodological, and developmental synthesis of integrated and biologically related factors.

I develop my argument to the theory of the crime-as-choice theory originally developed by Neal Shover (1998), Shover & Hochstetler (2005) and Shover, Hochstetler & Alalehto (2012). The crime-as-choice theory represents both an integrative and multi-methodological theory. First of all, the theory combines sociology (the structure of social action) with organizational theory (the organizational structure for choosing) and cognitive psychology (the structure of decision-making) into one coherent theory about what specific conditions is needed for a person to choose white collar crime. Secondly, the theory expresses the multi-methodological approach through integrating institutional, organizational and individual levels into one model. This method allows the capacity to consider the variation in crime rate (in a specific area/time period/industry) correlated with the variation of decision-making conditioned by the organizational frame and the opportunity structure for individuals to make a criminal decision. The third aspect of the crime-as-choice theory is that it integrates different criminological theories such as the theory of routine activity, choice theory, theories of social learning, crime pattern theories, and cognitive psychological studies.

The crime-as-choice theory presents an argument as to why a certain group of individuals chooses white collar crime. The theory proposes an integrated model of factors working on different levels. For example, the lack of credible oversight on an aggregated level, the existence of a crime-facilitative culture on an organizational level, and some certain propensities as aggressiveness, thrill-seeking, resilience, and entitlement on an individual level leading to the realization of criminal opportunities. The concepts and the causal structure of crime-as-choice theory will be more specifically presented below.

However, as a typical social scientific theory the crime-as-choice theory lacks a complete etiological argument behind its proposed proximate causality. I will elaborate upon the etiological concepts by applying arguments from the fields of evolutionary theory and biologically related criminology. I will then use institutional theory to discuss fraud and the function of fraudulent behavior in crime-as-choice theory so that the theory gets an even more coherent structure between ultimate and proximate causes[1].

In section I, a presentation of the recent research into evolutionary theory is given, where the discussion is focused on deceitful behavior such as cheating and its further implications in white collar crime. In section II, a deductive model on fraud is presented, which is based on the previous discussion on the mechanisms behind fraudulent action within contemporary evolutionary theory. Lastly, in section III, I will exemplify my model by applying it to the crime-as-choice theory, thus giving the theory a constitutional background of ultimate causes and showing how these causes are intertwined into the theories own assumptions of the proximal causes behind crime.

---

[1] Ultimate cause refers in this particular chapter to a cheater which receives the benefits from a mutually oriented cooperator without paying back. The cheater gets thereby more resources to survive and to improve his position as a resource strong organism in the competition of sexual selection, than if he had not got the benefits from the mutually beneficent cooperator. The mutually beneficent cooperator for its part spend his time and energy on activities that does not improve his survive or reproducing capacity in the sexual selection competition. Proximate causes refers for example to liquidity problems for the cheater to behold a certain kind of financial and social status, by cheating anyone else who holds the resources to solve the status problem for the cheater which may lead the deceived to get into liquidity problems instead (Scott-Phillips, Dickins, & West, 2011).

I. The Discussion among Evolutionary Theorists and Biosocial Criminologists on Deceit As an Etiological Structure for Criminological Theories on Fraud

The most prominent example of an etiological theory on deceitfulness and cheating is through the perspective of evolutionary theory. In the field of evolutionary psychology we can find an explanation of how the evolutionary mechanisms behind cheating functions and how these mechanisms can be used to consider the motivation behind why individuals commit fraud. The evolutionary psychologists show us both the ultimate cause behind why individuals choose to cheat as well as providing us with a credible explanation as to why there are individual variances within the levels of one's deceitfulness.

The essential evolutionary element to deceitful behavior is when the perpetrator receives a benefit from another individual but fails to reimburse him for it equitably. In current evolutionary theory cheating is treated as a fundamental problem which conflicts with the self-interest of all individuals. When an individual does something for someone else without receiving a reward of equal value, it means that the former loses the whole value of his deed and in the long run negates the possibility of reproducing himself successfully. Therefore an action must be followed by a counter-action, since anything else would be a conflict of self-interest (Dawkins 1992; Trivers, 2002). In the long-run the consequence would be that all kinds of self-sacrificial labor would collapse in the struggle for day-to-day existence and the species would be headed for extinction (Barrett, Dunbar, & Lycett, 2002; Waal, 2005; Waal, 1996).

The theoretical basis for reproductive self-interest is found in the work of biologist William Hamilton (1964). Hamilton argued that there are two fundamental ways in which an organism can reproduce itself. Either the organism takes the matter into its own hands and consistently produces offspring or it assists and supports the reproductive process for its descendants and nearest relatives. This theory claims that the closer the kinship is than the more willing the donor will be to give some of his resources to his offspring (fifty per cent of the genes). There is less willingness proportionately as the degree of kinship (inclusive fitness) diminishes. For example, the same action may require two cousins (25 per cent of the genes) or four cousin children (12.5 per cent of the genes) and so on. For more distant relatives the figure has to increase considerably to make the overall scheme rational from a genetic standpoint. What Hamilton postulates is the altruistic point of departure for which the donor does not demand any compensation; it is sufficient that the donor's genes successfully reproduces themselves for future generations (Dawkins 1992). The closer the kinship, the stronger and more self-sacrificial the deed of solidarity, while the weaker the kinship bond is, the less solidarity.[2] Of course, a lot of daily social exchanges takes place between non-related individuals where a successful reproductive strategy is uncertain for the donor. What makes this possible? The evolutionary theorist Robert Trivers (1971) proposed the concept of "reciprocal altruism"[3] to explain the evolutionary function of social exchange between strangers. Reciprocal helping involves a time delayed test of trust, loyalty and solidarity between unrelated individuals where the receiver gets the profit and the donor makes the sacrifice in their exchange with the idea that if I share some of my resources with you today, you will share some of your resources with me tomorrow. This theory involves the question of social control between two parts through deciding if the other individual is a friend or an enemy.[4]

Fraud As an Anti-Social Strategy

Yet, practicing reciprocal helping can be difficult when deciding the credibility of the other party in a social exchange. It does not give a precise description of the mechanism[5] behind the process. This concerns the nature of

---

[2] More strictly speaking, according to West, El Mouden, & Gardner (2011), this view of inclusive fitness is quit not altruism. When the acts are beneficial for both parts (the actor and the recipient) it is mutually beneficent, not altruistic. An altruistic act is when it is costly for the actor but beneficial for the recipient.

[3] According to West, et al. (2011) this is not a correct terminology. What Trivers describes is mutually beneficent for both parts. West et.al, prefer instead "reciprocal helping" as an act of direct reciprocity. I will follow their terminology concerning these particular concepts.

[4] One opinion about this phenomena is that humans have an algorithm for social contract specialized in calculating input and output of social exchanges through a 'cheating detector' whose sole purpose is to unmask deceit when a time-delayed social exchange takes place. This algorithm is universal, unitary and independent of cultural variation in all its form (Barkow, 1992; Cosmides & Tooby, 2005). A contradictory opinion for a cheating detector is that cheating is more a product of our plasticity and environmental conditions for how it functions in human nature (Buller 2000). This issue is still an open question (Scott-Phillips m.fl., 2011), even if there are some empirical evidence pointing out the existence of an algorithm (Bell & Buchner, 2012).

[5] Of course in the discussion of evolutionary stable strategies which is strategies that cannot be invaded by another strategies, the Tit for Tat is a well-known mechanism. TfT refers to the

pro-sociality, such as our natural selected social emotions where we intrinsically feel anger for being cheated or feel guilt or shame when considering whether to cheat someone. We want to feel empathy, sympathy, love and gratitude from others and we want to encourage cooperation when we need help solving adaptive problems for ourselves. In all, this gives a pro-social adaptive strategy for reproduction for the individuals, producing a societal structure that exceeds each contribution made towards it (Wiebe, 2012). Through this assumption we can suggest that those individuals who do not genetically share the same quality of social emotions will adapt an anti-social strategy for successful reproduction. These are the psychopaths and sociopaths, with two different causal mechanisms, often engaged in deceitful activities (Walsh & Wu, 2008).

Although rare (about 2%), there is a type of psychopath in the population throughout human societies where deceitfulness is the standard (Walsh & Wu, 2008). Psychopaths seem to be genetically predisposed for anti-social behavior, but the proportion of psychopaths is frequency-dependent, i.e. small numbers of psychopaths can be a relative successful way to reproduce itself in relation to the percentage of the predominant pro-social individuals in the milieu (Yao, Långström, Temrin, & Walum, 2014). But if, theoretically, the psychopaths should become predominant in the population, all aspects of reciprocal helping and cooperative interactions would break down and any kind of social exchange would be impossible (Walsh & Wu, 2008). However, as observations of representative samples of children and adults in experiments show, cooperation and the predisposition to cheat is evenly divided between individuals (Trivers 1971), in which the general population will cheat to some extent without crossing the border to become known as a persistent cheater. However, for sociopaths, their predisposition to cheat is not linked so strongly to genetics as it is for psychopaths (Mealey, 1995). Instead the causality for a sociopath is determined through both environmental factors of learned deviant behavior through bad parenting and a loose connection to deviant genetic properties transferred from the parents to the offspring. That is, it's more of a sustained causality than determined causality when sociopath inherit genes which makes them vulnerable for antisocial behavior and at the same time is raised in a home environment with role models who facilitate the traits of their genes into a criminal behavior. Overall, there should be more sociopaths in the society than psychopaths and, compared to psychopaths, sociopaths should

strategy when a cooperating player respond in the same direction as the other player choose to take with reference to the first initial move (Axelrod & Hamilton, 1981).

vary significantly in number within society as they are more dependent on external conditions such as the frequency of abuse, neglect, harm and life of poverty (Walsh & Wu, 2008).

Sociopaths and psychopaths choose an antisocial strategy based on different causal mechanisms. The question is why do they choose an anti-social strategy rather than a pro-social strategy? One explanation is that an individual who take the direction of an antisocial strategy is not competitive in the pro-social arena. They cannot reproduce themselves successfully on the pro-social arena so they have to challenge it with a competitive disadvantaged model for successful procreation (Wiebe, 2012). However, the main point here, especially for the sociopaths, is that they choose a competitive disadvantaged model both for economic and personal reasons. That is, their experience of poverty, strain, anomie, alienation or abuse by those in power along with their innate propensity for risk-taking, impulsivity, egocentrism, and shortsightedness causes them to be hostile towards society (Wiebe, 2012). This type of sociopath can be said to represent most of the street criminals and low-level fraudsters.

Sociopath As a Successful Fraud Strategy

So what is the origin of the sociopath that becomes a more powerful white collar criminal? According to Wiebe (2012), an alternative path to offending is the competitive advantage model. This models points out the classic Machiavellian thesis: if you are powerful enough then you can get away with anything. This is based on the assumption that a certain kind of sociopath (or even psychopath) will have high self-control but will feel little empathy, guilt, and remorse and will be very egocentric (see also Babiak, Neumann, & Hare, 2010). This kind of offender will behave deceptively partly because the relationship with the victim is short-term with little risk of encountering the victim again in future (Nettle & Dunbar 1997). They are also displaced from the victim, both physically and psychologically. They may also rationalize their criminality to themselves and to others by neutralization techniques and account-giving. Wiebe does not give any further explanation what the mechanism behind this process can be, more than it is "…individuals in possession of inadequately checked power. " (ibid: 355).

In fact, Wiebe's description of a sociopath can be clarified through the concept of resource holding potential presented by Cohen & Machalek (1988:471) which explicitly refers to white collar criminals (ibid: 482).

Resource holding potential refers to the organism's chances of producing offspring which survive to reproductive age, where the exercise of power serves as a potential resource for the sociopath. This is also described through Charles Tittles (1995, 2004) concept of *imbalanced control ratio*: If the offender experiences an imbalance between his ability to control the environment (control surplus) relative to the amount he feels controlled, he will have an imbalanced control ratio of 2:0 and it is predicted that he will commit crime. This imbalance is explained to reduce the amount of humiliation that he feels through being controlled, which at the same time can serve as a legitimate reason to behave in accordance to the competitive advantage model. That is, the sense of humiliation contributes to the offender's need to reinforce his surplus control and increase his autonomy as a resourceful individual.

Cohen and Machalek's, and Tittle's, arguments indicate roughly a gene-environment interaction (GxE). That is, environmental risk factors in themselves do not explain much of individual variance of criminality, but if the individual has a biological risk factor and grow up in a threatening environments then involvement into criminality raises significantly (Mealey, 1995). The concept of GxE has recently been developed to developmental GxE interaction, were the capacity of learning abilities among the individuals as phenotypes gives a variety in results depending on how the environmental stimuli interplay with the genotypic shaped construction of cell assemblies within the individual (Rutter, 2010; Tabery, 2007). For example, normal conditioned environmental stimuli (presence of parenting, friendship, average income, etc) is sufficient to permit building functioning cell assemblies at a majority of individuals, i.e. to behave as conformist probably because they harbor a set of alleles[6] who controls up their behavior to become conformist. But the same conditioned environmental stimuli is not enough to permit building functioning cell assemblies at delinquent individuals, because the environmental stimuli has either the quality or the magnitude to impact the phenotypic construction of cell assemblies at the delinquent individual, because they probably harbor a set of risk alleles which does not controls up their behavior.[7] However, the environmental stimuli can affect this phenotypic shaped construction of cell assemblies if the environment stimuli is enriched

[6] That is, the variety of all the genes or a specific set of genes. An allele is constituted by the RNA and proteins which in its whole constitute the individual and gives the unique properties of the individual.

[7] In other words, this is polymorphism where you have a variety in the same population of the specie.

(e.g. loving and caring parenting, disposal and encouraging friendship, above average income, etc) for the delinquent individual which is enough to turn him to be conformist. Whilst the same enriched environmental stimuli has no significant effect on the construction of cell assemblies at the already conformist individual.[8]

Recently research in molecular genetics show that there is a genetic variety of risk alleles among the population of phenotypes (Beaver & Connolly, 2013; Simons & Lei, 2013). There is a continuum by phenotypes who hold an amount of risk alleles to phenotypes who shows none or just a few risk alleles, where the majority of the population harbor a normal distribution of risk alleles. The issue of risk alleles has a specific significance toward criminality if the risk alleles is concentrated to the following genes which are correlated to antisocial behavior: MAO-A, DRD2, DRD4, COMT, DAT1 (genes connected to the neurotransmitter Dopamine which stimulate reward and sensations seeking); 5-HTT (a gen connected to punishment and dissatisfying) and GABA holding the genes GABRA2, GABRG1, which impact the general condition of disinhibition and excitability in the brain (Beaver & Connolly, 2013). If the risk alleles is viewed as a plastic property, the specific phenotype who holds an amount of risk alleles shows a variation in behavior depending on what kind of good or bad environment condition the specific phenotype is exposed of. If the phenotype is exposed of good environment condition (e.g. loving and caring parenting, caring siblings, disposal and encouraging friendship, etc) it responds positive by not triggering the risk alleles (which is hold back) so the phenotype responds with conformity in its behavior (Simons & Kit Lei, 2013).

What we can suspect is that the variation in environmental conditions who potentially triggers/none triggers the risk alleles, especially concerning sociopaths, can be the etiological structure behind why specifically white collar criminals perform as late bloomers (mean age of 41-42 year) with no particular criminal history (Alalehto & Larsson, 2008; M. L. Benson, 2002; Bussmann & Werle, 2006; Gottschalk, 2013; K. Holtfreter, Van Slyke, & Blomberg, 2005; Kardell & Bergqvist, 2009; Kerley & Copes, 2004; Onna, Geest, Huisman, & Denkers, 2014; Poortinga, Lemmen, & Jibson, 2006;

[8] My example is an analogy to an example retrieved from Tabery (2007:973). Another path to think about this GxE interplay is that some individuals have a genotype which is non-sensitive for all kind of environmental stimuli despite quality and magnitude (they can only be helped by pharmacological treatment), whilst other individuals has a genotype which is sensitive for all kind of environmental stimuli (who can be helped by therapeutic treatment) (Rutter, 2010).

Soothill, Humphreys, & Francis, 2012; Weisburd, 1991; Weisburd m.fl., 2001; Wheeler, Weisburd, Waring, & Bode, 1988). The suggestion is that late bloomers in general is confronted by bad environmental conditions at their middle age which trigger their risk alleles (Krohn, Gibson, & Thornberry, 2013). We do know that there are some specific bad environmental conditions which correlate with white collar criminality on the individual level. That is a higher divorce rate than among street criminals and the general population (Alalehto & Larsson, 2008; Klenowski, Copes, & Mullins, 2010; Walters & Geyer, 2004; Weisburd, 1991), which is especially the case among female white collar offenders (Daly, 1989; Haantz, 2002; Shechory, Perry, & Addad, 2011). And we also know that white collar criminals suffer from at least one emotional, marital, or substance abuse problem over the course of their lives (Weisburd, 1991; Soothill et al., 2012). Where around 7% of low-frequency offenders have problems with drug abuse and around 5% have alcohol abuse problems (Onna et.al., 2014; Weisburd m.fl., 2001), which is a higher rate of substance abuse than the general population (Poortinga m.fl., 2006). Another interesting issue with regard to health problems is the observation that tax evaders in Sweden have a slightly higher mortality rate than the general population. This difference is clearly gendered, were convicted female tax offenders have a 2% higher mortality rate than the general population and male tax offenders (Ring, 2003).

However, if we go back to the discussion of molecular genetics and its relation to white collar crime research, Beaver & Holtfreter show that the MAO-A[9] has in itself a significant negative association to fraud. But if the individual has a criminal father there is a significant positive association to fraud. In addition, if this individual also has a high-functioning MAO-A (3.5, 4 and 5-paired allele[10]) the regression odds increase significantly for crime. By a split-sample model, Beaver & Holtfreter (2009) applied a high- and low-delinquent peer sample. The results showed that none of the covariates (race, age, family situation, or parents' experience of crime) were statistically associated to the potential for someone to commit fraud for the low-delinquent peer sample, and that MAO-A had a negative significant association to fraud even for the high-delinquent peer sample. However, involvement in high-

[9] That is, monoamine oxidase A, which regulate the neurotransmitters of serotonin, dopamine and norepinephrine which have been found to be linked to delinquency and criminal behavior.

[10] See Beaver et al., (2013) which is a opposite result compared to violent offenders, see Caspi et al., (2002) who shows that individuals with low-functioning MAO-A (2 or 3-paired alleles) have an increased odds ratio for violence.

delinquent peer sample with a high-functioning MAO-A showed a significant risk for fraud which means that an individual with high-functioning MAO-A conditioned by high-delinquent peers become a full-scale fraudster.

Beaver & Holtfreter study is a good starting point to understand the developmental GxE interaction behind powerful fraudsters, but they still have only shown the correlations of a general interaction, not the causality of it. Further research on this topic would be desirable to develop a step-by-step scheme of the mechanisms of fraud (or any other particular white collar crime) in the way as Caspi et al. (2002) theorize:

1) An individual has a risk allele in the MAO-A.
2) The neurotransmitters used by the brain cells cannot sufficiently be degraded by the MAO-A which instead is stored in the brain.
3) Communication between brains cells deteriorate.
4) The person has difficulty in handling stress-filled situations.
5) The person cannot relax and cope with the situation but "over-reacts" with aggression.
6) Long period of excessively high levels of MAO-A change the brain and establish aggression as a mode of adaptation.
7) This in turn finds expression in situations where the person experiences carelessness or ill-treatment.

There is no similar description of the mechanism of fraud presented so far in the field.

II. The Evolutionary Logic Behind Fraud

Based on the preceding argument of how fraud functions, I suggest the following preliminary model which provides a step-by-step description of fraudulent behavior:

a) Humans work on the belief that each new social relationship is based on a reciprocal confidence in each other, until the opposite is proven.
b) Cheating is a means for successful reproduction, which is transmitted genetically through mating selection by the phenotypes.
c) The degree of successful reproduction by cheating is on an aggregated level frequency-depended, but can on the individual level vary rather

substantially by those phenotypes with an amount of risk alleles for cheating to those who has none or just few risk alleles for cheating.

d) Those phenotypes who harbor an amount of risk alleles which are triggered by bad environmental conditions is predisposed to perform as cheaters.
e) The more the social relationship toward a predisposed cheater depends on a time-delayed reciprocal confidence, the higher the degree of manipulation will occur from the cheaters part.
f) The higher the degree of anonymity and the lower the degree of social control there is in the society, the greater the possibilities for false reciprocal confidence will occur. This will lead to a higher degree of fraudulent action from the predisposed cheater.
g) Finally the more powerful the predisposed cheater is, the more likely it is that he use *e* and *f* as conditions to hide his actions from others.

The causality of this model is dependent on the fact that *a* and *b* are two general rules from evolutionary theory which state that reciprocity is the general principle for humans when creating a social relationship, and cheating is one successful means for reproduction. The following criteria for *c* are more of a particular kind of rule deduced from *a* and *b* where *d* follows from *c* in its turn. The criterion of *c* rests on the distribution of risk alleles in the population were criterion *d* describes the sub-population of cheaters who harbor an amount of risk alleles combined with bad environmental conditions which give them a capacity to cheat by false intentions in their social relations. The criterion for *e* is then specified to situations on an individual level where the social relations is time-delayed between giving and counter-giving. And the criterion of *f* is a complement to *e* laying on aggregated level describing the loss of intimacy in the social relations which give the cheater a degree of freedom to act fraudulent. Finally the criterion of *g* is the deduced hypotheses from *a*, *b*, *c*, *d*, *e* and *f* which can be tested empirically on defined places or variation in crime rate on individual and aggregate level.

The criterion *e* can be seen in societies where there has been an increase over time of service industries in proportion to manufacturing industries (Gratzer, 2001; Alalehto & Larsson, 2009). Specifically in these kinds of service industries there exist a time-delayed social relationship, such as between the salesman and buyer, which is mediated by long-distance and impersonal ways, such as internet correspondence and online transactions. Another example of this type of social relationship is when parties use attorneys to communicate. This kind of relationship is especially vulnerable to fraud as it is built on trust, loyalty and personal confidence, like the creditor-debtor relationship. These circumstances give the deduction of criteria *f*: If the degree of anonymity increases (as an effect of a long-distance relationship) and the capacity for social control decreases (from the effect of non-physical interactions and claiming non-responsibility), the chances will increase for deceitful individuals to commit fraud with confidence. Criteria *g* is then deduced from *e* and *f* where the degree of powerful resources of the single offender counts as an important factor to hide his intentions for others control. The criteria of *e* and *f* can also counts for physical interactions were a potential powerless fraudster may lull the victim into security by giving the impression that everything is fine.

III. The Application of the Evolutionary Logic Behind Fraud in the Crime-As-Choice Theory

The proposals of the evolutionary working mechanism can be connected to more environmentally proximal causes of social mechanism. I will henceforth argue how this evolutionary working mechanism is connected to the social mechanism that the crime-as-choice theory is comprised of.

The crime-as-choice theory specifies demographic, social and cultural mechanisms accordingly to the opportunity structure of constraints and possibilities capturing the analytical level of individuals up to the analytical level of crime rate variation between countries. Especially criteria *d, e* and *f* up to the conclusive criteria of *g* is getting much more body if they are developed into the concepts presented by the crime-as-choice theory.

The crime-as-choice theory states the following conceptual structure. It is a choice theory, but it does not state a priori that criminal choices are rational like rational choice theory does. In general, the theory states that humans makes choices in their daily lives and in every opportunity there are different options. Some people are lured to different options, in which they may see an opportunity out of committing crime. The theory further states that the lure vary generally between different opportunities because of the level of credible external oversight (monitoring and surveillance systems) and the level of different prohibiting internal oversight (conscience among individuals, internal governance in organizations and the crime-facilitative culture in the context). In every kind of monitoring system there is a an absence in some sense of capable guardians, which depend on the complexity of properties involved in any opportunity where trust is constituted, giving the individual a chance to define the situation as a criminal opportunity.

But not every one of us is going to define an opportunity as a criminal opportunity. In fact the theory stipulates that there are a group of individuals predisposed to creating and taking advantage of these potential opportunities and define them as criminal opportunities. These individuals are defined both by a between-group characterization and a within-individual characterization in the way that these predisposed individuals are featured by some social properties (competence and skills) and cultural experiences (knowledge) which they use in particular opportunities. These features separate them from every other individual who lacks the same qualities of social and cultural experiences. Combined with this, these individuals show a propensity to be morally ambivalent, resilient, thrill-seeking, self-restrained, arrogant and entitled.

The causal structure can then be understood as: In a case where an opportunity presents itself and temps an offender, and the opportunity lacks credible oversight, then it can be viewed as a criminal opportunity. However, it can only be realized as a crime-scene if the offender identifies that the temptation is worth taking advantage of as a criminal opportunity trigged by his propensities. The proximal mechanism is here clearly identified starting with lure which draws the attention, after which in the next step favor the attraction of the predisposed / tempted individuals to favor the opportunity as a specified criminal opportunity lacking credible external and effective prohibiting internal oversight.

The General Distribution of Fraudsters According to Empirical Investigations

However, in the real world the frequency in which one feels this temptation will vary between different opportunities and so will the capacity of effective internal and credible external oversight do as well as the frequency of cross passing predisposed / tempted individuals (henceforth referred to as psychopaths/sociopaths) will do.

For these purposes, it is easier to speak about groups of psychopaths and sociopaths as a heterogenic group consisting of at least three kinds of offender profiles: the stereotypical offender, the opportunity seeker and the crises responder (Weisburd, 1991; Piquero & Weisburd 2009). Stereotypical offenders are similar to persistent offenders who define an opportunity as a criminal opportunity regardless of whether the opportunity has an effective prohibiting internal or credible external oversight. The frequency of stereotypical offenders (psychopaths) should be stable over time. Opportunity seekers (sociopaths) are also persistent offenders who will react to temptation with eagerness and respond to the strength of credible oversight by searching for opportunities where prohibiting internal or credible external oversight is lacking in some way. Opportunity seekers should be stable over time and situations. Crises responders, i.e. Machiavellian personalities with a moderate phenotypic predisposition of risk alleles for cheating, reacts to situational factors at given moments (so called 'interactionism' or 'human agency', see McGuire, 2004; Mealey, 1995; Walsh & Wu, 2008). These makes up the majority of white collar criminals. They will look for opportunities in which they feel they can take advantage of when they have a temporary surplus control over the situation. The frequency of crises responders will depend more on changes in institutional factors (such as economic downturn, rapid technological shifts, incentives given by political reforms or jurisdictional changes) than their within-individual properties. They should respond to credible internal or external oversight of a situation.

Several cluster investigations based on attitudinal and self-reported criminality have indicated a similar kind of distribution of potential offenders in the same proportion as the above cluster analysis of Piquero & Weisburd. In general, 3-5 clusters have been reported concerning tax crime and insurance fraud. A rather typical proportion of the clusters are presented by Dean (2004).

Dean's research contained the following questions: Does the person perceive all types of insurance fraud as a violation toward morality (49% of the sample)? Does the person feel that insurance fraud is a moral violation, but to some degree they could understand its grounds (32.4%)? Does the person have a more tolerant perception of insurance fraud as neither morally wrong or right (10.8%)? Finally, does the person perceive insurance fraud as morally acceptable, fair and just towards the insurance companies/agents (7.8%)? Similar results have been reported (Babakus, Cornwell, Mitchell, & Schlegelmilch, 2004; Brinkmann & Lentz, 2006; Jay, 1997; Larsson & Alalehto, 2013) with a rather high proportion of morally restrictive attitudes toward white collar crime through a continuum to a small sample of liberal attitudes accepting nearly all kinds of white collar crime. Almost the same proportional results have also been reported in clustered self-reported white collar criminality.

The economists Wärneryd & Walerud (1982) identified 3 clusters of people associated with tax (tax evaders, 17.5%; regular tax payers 44.5%; tax planners, 38%) in Sweden. Those who admitted tax evasion had a (on a 5% level) pro-gambling stance towards tax evasion (they would take the chance to reduce their tax illegally) and felt the tax system was unfair (the taxation system was experienced as unjust) which was contrary to regular tax payers and tax planners.

Tennyson (2002) compared the attitudes of self-reported insurance fraud with tax crime and found that if the individual felt it okay to not report some income share to the IRS, there was also a 50% risk that he would also feel it was okay to commit insurance fraud. The crucial factors for this distribution were primarily the individual's social and ethical milieu such as the acceptance for insurance and tax fraud among the individual's peer-group. Secondary to this was the individual's general sense of justice about whether it was okay to cheat IRS or not. The third circumstance was the individual's own experience about cheating an insurance company when they had an experience of a company cheating them first. On the other hand, Tennyson (2002) found that individuals who had a positive experience of the insurance industry did not found it acceptable to commit insurance fraud.

These cluster investigations helps us to empirically identify the amount of potential psychopaths (e.g. liberals), sociopaths (e.g., tolerant, evaders), and Machiavellian (e.g. sympathetic) individuals and their attitudes towards morally restrictive (non-offending) individuals. The investigations address the variety of attitudes that people share toward white collar crime and the correlation between acceptance of crime and how crime is self-reported. These results can, to some extent, be explained by the theory of crime-as-choice through the group of tempted offenders equipped with varying resources of competence, skills, and experience. But it is an explanation that stops at proximate causes.

The Main Etiological Point

What I wish to establish within the crime-as-choice theory is the driving force behind the social propensities of people who act egoistically and take advantage of opportunities in order to satisfy their self-interest. These propensities include arrogance, narcissism, and entitlement. This in contrast to other humans who are predisposed to behave altruistically with cooperation and reciprocity as their main goal. Between these two extremes is a continuum from extreme egoism (psychopath and sociopath) to altruism, as the above cluster investigations show.

The question is then, how can this continuum between biological factors and environmental factors be understood? Once again we have to look at the indications that link biological factors with environmental factors. One starting point is the results that Beaver & Holtfreter (2009) present and the idea of a competitive advantage model presented by Wiebe (2012). Through choosing a competitive advantage model we can suspect that white collar offenders should have a high level of self-control, such as being self-employed, investing in education, being married, receiving a regular income and being regularly employed. They would also deny any kind of wrongdoings or illegal acts (because of their psychopathic nature), until the opposite is proven. In fact, much of the demographic research shows that the majority of white collar criminals are middle class, self-employed, married, and well educated with a high income, regardless of time-era and context (Alalehto & Larsson, 2008, 2012; Benson & Simpson, 2009; Weisburd et al., 2001; Weisburd, 1991; Wheeler, Weisburd, Waring, & Bode, 1988). It is also stated that they do not acknowledge their crime and will continuously deny it, or argue with excuses or try to justify their crime (Benson & Walker, 1988; Benson, 1985; Copes, 2003; Jacobsson, 2011; Klenowski, Copes, & Mullins, 2010; Minor, 1981; Rothman & Gandossy, 1982; Shover, Coffey, & Hobbs, 2003).

We also know that white collar criminals show a higher intelligence than street criminals (Raine et al., 2012) and that their personality traits are relatively homogenously distributed to be extroverted, hedonistic, non-agreeable and Machiavellian egocentric (Alalehto, 2003; Blickle, Schlegel, Fassbender, & Klein, 2006; Feeley, 2006; Listwan, Piquero, & Van Voorhis, 2010). Both of these latter factors are GxE connected with a mean split between genetics and peer-group influenced effects.

Overall, we can conclude that there should be a rather sophisticated developmental GxE interaction between high-delinquency peers and high-functioning MAO-A developing psychopaths/sociopaths who show high self-control, eccentric personality traits with a high IQ-level and a denial of crime. The question is how this developmental GxE interaction could be understood in more etiological details for white collar criminals?

One starting point is genetic strategies transmitted by inheritance for sociopathic and psychopathic personalities affecting their decision-making. But that's just one part of the story. If we consider the psychopath his biological predispositions serves only as a base, acting as an agent in an environment he has to learn through classic and operant conditioning what kind of actions reinforces his outcomes positively or negatively. This developmental strategy of learning abilities serves in its turn as a base for invention and innovation on how the psychopath handles particular situations. Developmental strategies are a link between genes and environment, but they are limited to single individuals as an analytical unit. The complexity of crime patterns occur when they are extended to apply to a collective phenomenon, as groups and communities. This makes sub-cultures and organizations as an analytical unit. Even on this level the developmental GxE interaction can meet the criteria if it is understood as cultural strategies, such as it is described by Cohen & Machalek (1988). They describe them as aggregated processes of communication and social learning (imitation and socialization) by which the individual learns and confirms the criminal strategies from others.

This idea is well known in criminology as social learning of pro-criminality contending techniques, definitions and values of justification of crime irrespective if the processes are percept as reinforcement (Akers, 2009) or modeling (Sutherland, 1985). That is, cultural strategies are extensively developed in the theory of social disorganization, concerning crime patterns in certain communities in contrast to other communities (Shaw & McKay, 1969).

A Reversed and Complemental Etiology

This model becomes significantly more complicated if we introduce institutionalized strategies as a fourth dimension. Institutionalized strategies means that the culture itself is governed and regulated by some overall norms steering the forms and content of the individuals capacity to communicate and socially learn 'the rules of the game' in more wider social contexts. Depending on how the institutional regulation develops over time, it will affect the cultural strategies. If we consider that the institutional regulation is weak then it brings no confidence for the 'rules of the game', where regulation will bring more disorganization. This affects the community values and societal norms. On the contrary, if the institutional regulation is strong it will help individuals organize their lives. However, when the institutional regulation is weak, criminal decision-making can be the first options by individuals to make sense over their lives. This causes the crime rate to increase. How an institution regulates itself develops over time, and it affects the magnitude of individuals to choose crime. It is important to note that this overwhelming institutional regulation will serve as an ultimate cause for criminality (Rosenfeld &

Messner, 2013).[11] Institutional strategies are much weaker in relation to the gene structure[12] and of course much stronger concerning environmental dimensions.

This argument gives a rather complicated configuration on how we can understand the causality between independent conditions and crime as a dependent variable. Analytically the developmental GxE interaction shows a conditional causality. The gene serves as a blueprint for behavior, including fraudulent behavior. There is some direct causality between inheritance (a high-functioning MAO-A) and crime (committing fraud). But it describes only a small amount of offenders. Mostly the causal relationship between genes and criminality is mediated by a couple of proximate causes as socially-learned reinforcement (RF), the involvement in delinquent peer-groups, affecting their IQ and personality traits and thereby giving the individual the propensities and cognitive capacities of skill, experience and competence acting in particular opportunities. This latter process is then moderated by the crime-facilitative culture (in the community, group or organization) impacting the level of skill, experience and competence to flourish depending on the structure of communication and societal norms and values in the community.

This argument shows causality, conditioned from genes to crime, mediated by environmental factors. The problem is then that institutional regulations (which also are a conditional cause) will in turn effect the population on an aggregated level to regulate the variation in magnitude whether individuals choose crime.

One can consider the links between institutional regulation and frequency-dependent genetic dispositions, albeit it is far-fetched, through Willem Bonger's (1969) theory on the fraudulent nature of capitalism. Bonger claimed that the core of white collar criminality lay on the economic conditions determined by the capitalistic mode of production. Capitalism caused a breed of egoism which damaged the core of egalitarianism in society, where everything and everyone could be exploited and exchanged in order to make

[11] Which of course is something else then the ultimate cause idea associated to natural selection. For a clarification see Scott-Phillips m.fl. (2011) and (West m.fl., 2011). However, ultimate cause in this particular meaning refers to the standard Durkhemian model in Sociology, that social facts explain why the behavior of agents (individuals, groups, collectives) takes a certain performances defined by the given institutional structure of the social system.

[12] However Beaver & Wright (2011) show a significant correlation between IQ and crime rate on county-level. If the aggregated IQ is high the aggregated crime rate becomes low, and vice versa. But this study is limited too property and violent crime and is not discussing any eventual correlation between aggregated level of IQ and aggregated level of white collar criminality.

profits for the exploiter (see also Currie, 2013 and Coleman, 1987 for similar arguments). This egocentric tendency of capitalism is seen when the exploiters' counterpart show a weak side, as in the case of desperate workers whose labor power is underpaid and exploited by the capitalist, or by merchants who see every chance to cheat a weak counterpart. Based on these we could see how institutions constitute the home base for powerful Machiavellian personality types, and sociopaths, where the rate of capitalistic egoism affects the rate of Machiavellianism in the market.

Regardless, institutional regulation gives an aggregated causality, which theoretically goes in reverse direction toward the genetic etiology. In the end it gives two kinds of ultimate causes behind the 'why' of white collar crime.

The following figure[13] is presented to illustrate these arguments. Crime is put in the middle of the model (as a dependent variable) caused as phenomena by two independently ultimate causes, which do not affect each other but do affect all mediating and moderating proximate causes in-between them toward crime.

The aggregated form of the ultimate cause behind crime is more easily explained in terms of the crimes-as-choice theory. Long-term variation as the inflation rate in society effects criminality in prevalence (Rosenfeld & Messner, 2013).

Higher prices lead to higher demands from the market of goods and services to compensate for the price fall for the companies. Those who not stand the test risk liquidity problems, which affect the incidence structure to commit crime in industries or single companies. Some companies come under greater pressure than others and become agents of fraud. Institutional regulation through inflation policy is important for individuals to trust institutions, affecting the organizational structure in how individuals will plan their future. Another important factor, as an example of short-term variation, is the rate and force of credibility in external oversight (law enforcement, agency control, industrial culture) affecting the deterrence and possibilities of defining normal situations as criminal opportunities by the offender (Shover et al., 2012). This factor deals with the question of resources and prioritization in politics. Resourceful agencies that prioritize white collar crime will be an institutional threat for active white collar offenders.

[13] I thank my colleague and partner in the study of crime, Daniel Larsson, for proposing the configuration of the model.

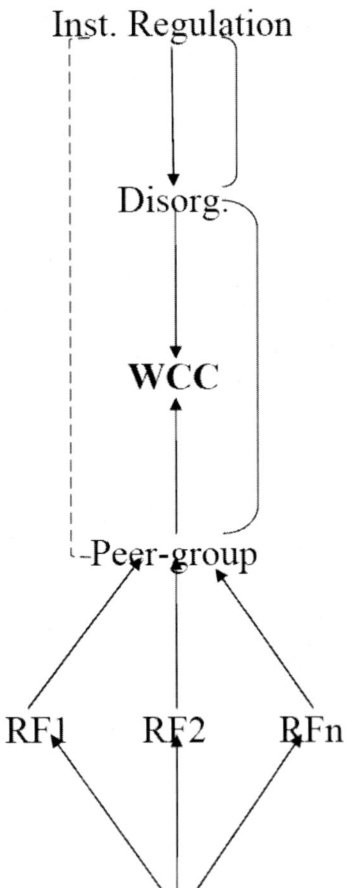

To conclude, the aim of this chapter was to argue for the possibility of using an integrated and biosocial approach into one single argument applied into the crime-as-choice theory. The method was to use an evolutionary based etiology to highlight the reasons behind the whole range of proximal causes as the crime-as-choice theory presents. This has led to the following theoretical hypothesis: Individuals predisposed to fulfill their egoism (psychopaths and sociopaths) will be more tempted to seek out temptation, look after non-credible oversight and define opportunities as criminal opportunities than normal offenders (Machiavellian) and non-offenders. This will have a direct effect on the number of instances of fraud being committed on an individual and organizational level, depending on the number of psychopaths and sociopaths in the industry at the time. Empirically this theoretical hypotheses means that we should have more white collar criminality, given the number of the pool of psychopath and sociopath, if there is an increase of anonymous long-distance financial relationships with a lack of credible oversight over time and/or the relationship between a debtor and creditor is mediated by a third socially uncontrolled part, resting on the quality of trust and affection.

The ultimate cause created by institutional regulation should show a sustainable causal effect on fraud depending on the variation of external societal factors such as the rate of inflation, recession, and credibility of external oversight, causing a disorganized culture impacting temporary offenders as Machiavellian personalities (and even normally non-offenders) to seek out temptation, look after non-credible oversight and define opportunities as criminal opportunities. In this latter form it would lead to a variation of the prevalence of fraud on both institutional and organizational level over time. Empirically this institutional aspect should lead to an increase of white collar criminality in times of high inflation and/or deep recessions and/or decrease of credible external oversight.

Conclusion

I have argued that criminological theories in general lack 'ultimate cause' explanations for their proposed structures of proximate causes as regards white-collar crime. I have taken the 'crime-as-choice' theory as a leading example in contemporary criminological theory of how an integration of two different ultimate causes by evolutionary biology and institutional regulation can be succeeded as a sliding scale to explain the variation of white-collar criminals from the pool of psychopaths to the pool of crises responders as it is presented by the theory of crime-as-choice. From evolutionary biology the idea of developmental gene-environment interaction (how genetic shaped construction combined with environmental stimuli affects the individual's behavior) and the competitive advantage model inspired by evolutionary psychology (how powerful egoism can be understood as a successful way of reproducing the individual's genes) provides an understanding of why there should be a rather stable frequency of predisposed/tempted white collar criminals regardless of time and place. From institutional regulation the idea of impacting aggregates as the rate of inflation, recession, political reforms, rapid technological shifts, credible oversight, etc affect the rules of the game in what way we can expect what will happen tomorrow.

This gives a variation in the frequencies of how many white collar criminals (crises responders) there are depending on whether the social conditions are organized or disorganized for these temporary tempted offenders.

Finally, from a perspective of crime prevention the number of psychopaths and sociopaths is very difficult to change. What can be done, even if it is limited, is to sharp the recruitment process by testing the psychological profiles of employees and thereby selecting out those who shows a psychopathic or sociopathic character before their entry into the industry. However, this cannot, to my knowledge, be done when it comes to employers. Another stake to be done, even if I do not know how, is to increase the inserts of social control into relationships with a delayed and long-distance relationship which is particularly vulnerable for fraud.

On an institutional level a desirable policy would be to hold down the rate of inflation, to avoid recession, to introduce more smoothly technological shifts, etc. If this could be possible to implement, it should have an impact on especially the majority of potential white collar criminals (crises responders) who would not come to a situation where they were pushed to consider a crime.

References

Agnew, R. (2004). Why do criminals offend? : a general theory of crime and delinquency. Los Angeles, Calif.: *Roxbury.*

Akers, R. (2009). Social Learning and Social Structure: A General Theory of Crime and Deviance. *Transaction Publishers.*

Alalehto, T. (2003). Economic Crime: Does Personality Matter? *International Journal of Offender Therapy and Comparative Criminology,* 47(3), 335 – 355. http://doi.org/10.1177/0306624X03047003007

Alalehto, T., & Larsson, D. (2008). Vem är den ekonomiske brottslingen? En sociodemografisk profilstudie av 23 länder. I T. Alalehto & D. Larsson (Reds), Den ljusskygga ekonomin: organiserad och ekonomisk brottslighet. Umeå: Umeå universitet.

Alalehto, T., & Larsson, D. (2009). The roots of modern white-collar crime : does the modern form of white-collar crime have its foundation in the transition from a society dominated by agriculture to one dominated by industry? *Critical Criminology*, 17(3), 183–193.

Alalehto, T., & Larsson, D. (2012). Who is the economic criminal? : A comparison between countries and types of crime. *Sociologisk Forskning*, 49(1), 25–44.

Axelrod, R., & Hamilton, W. D. (1981). The evolution of cooperation. Science, 211(4489), 1390–1396. http://doi.org/10.1126/science.7466396

Babakus, E., Cornwell, T. B., Mitchell, V., & Schlegelmilch, B. (2004). Reactions to unethical consumer behavior across six countries. Journal of Consumer Marketing, 21(4), 254–263. http://doi.org/10.1108/07363760410542165

Babiak, P., Neumann, C. S., & Hare, R. D. (2010). Corporate psychopathy: Talking the walk. *Behavioral Sciences & the Law,* 28(2), 174–193. http://doi.org/10.1002/bsl.925

Barkow, J. H. . C., Leda; Tooby, John. (1992). The dapted Mind: Evolutionary Psychology and the Generation of Culture. *Oxford University Press*, USA.

Barrett, L., Dunbar, R., & Lycett, J. (2002). Human evolutionary psychology. *Basingstoke: Palgrave.*

Beaver, K. M., Barnes, J. C., & Boutwell, B. B. (2014). The nurture versus biosocial debate in criminology: on the origins of criminal behavior and criminality.

Beaver, K. M., & Connolly, E. J. (2013). Genetic and Environmental Influences on the Development of Childhood Antisocial Behavior: Current Evidence and Directions for Future Research. I C. L. Gibson & M. D. Krohn (Reds), *Handbook of Life-Course Criminology* (ss 43–55). Springer New York. Hämtad från http://link.springer.com/chapter /10.1007/978-1-4614-5113-6_3

Beaver, K. M., & Holtfreter, K. (2009). Biosocial Influences on Fraudulent Behaviors. *The Journal of Genetic Psychology,* 170(2), 101–114. http://doi.org/10.3200/GNTP.170.2.101-114

Beaver, K. M., & Wright, J. P. (2011). The association between county-level IQ and county-level crime rates. *Intelligence,* 39(1), 22–26. http://doi.org/10.1016/j.intell.2010.12.002

Beaver, K. M., Wright, J. P., Boutwell, B. B., Barnes, J. C., DeLisi, M., & Vaughn, M. G. (2013). Exploring the association between the 2-repeat allele of the MAOA gene promoter polymorphism and psychopathic personality traits, arrests, incarceration, and lifetime antisocial behavior. *Personality and Individual Differences,* 54(2), 164–168. http://doi.org/10.1016/j.paid.2012.08.014

Bell, R., & Buchner, A. (2012). How Adaptive Is Memory for Cheaters? *Current Directions in Psychological Science,* 21(6), 403–408. http://doi.org/10.1177/0963721412458525

Benson, M. L. (1985). Denying the Guilty Mind: Accounting for Involvement in a White-Collar Crime*. Criminology, 23(4), 583–607. http://doi.org/10.1111/j.1745-9125.1985.tb00365.x

Benson, M. L. (2002). Crime and the life course : an introduction. Los Angeles, CA: Roxbury.

Benson, M. L., & Walker, E. (1988). Sentencing the White-Collar Offender. *American Sociological Review,* 53(2), 294–302.

Benson, M., & Simpson, S. (2009). White Collar Crime: An Opportunity Perspective (1a uppl). Routledge.

Blickle, G., Schlegel, A., Fassbender, P., & Klein, U. (2006). Some Personality Correlates of Business White-Collar Crime. *Applied Psychology,* 55(2), 220–233. http://doi.org/10.1111/j.1464-0597.2006.00226.x

Boisvert, D., Wright, J., Knopik, V., & Vaske, J. (nd). Genetic and Environmental Overlap between Low Self-Control and Delinquency. *Journal of Quantitative Criminology,* 1–31. http://doi.org/10.1007/s10940-011-9150-x

Bonger, W. (1969). Criminality and Economic Conditions. (First Edition. Hardback. Dust Jacket.). *Indiana University Press,.*

Brinkmann, J., & Lentz, P. (2006). Understanding Insurance Customer Dishonesty: Outline of a Moral-Sociological Approach. *Journal of Business Ethics,* 66(2-3), 177–195. http://doi.org/10.1007/s10551-005-5575-1

Bussmann, K.-D., & Werle, M. M. (2006). Addressing Crime in Companies. *British Journal of Criminology,* 46(6), 1128 –1144. http://doi.org/10.1093/bjc/azl072

Caspi, A., McClay, J., Moffitt, T. E., Mill, J., Martin, J., Craig, I. W., … Poulton, R. (2002). *Role of Genotype in the Cycle of Violence in Maltreated Children. Science,* 297(5582), 851–854. http://doi.org/10.1126/science.1072290

Cohen, L. E., & Machalek, R. (1988). A General Theory of Expropriative Crime: An Evolutionary Ecological Approach. *American Journal of Sociology,* 94(3), 465–501. http://doi.org/10.2307/2780251

Coleman, J. W. (1987). Toward an Integrated Theory of White-Collar Crime. *American Journal of Sociology,* 93(2), 406–439.

Copes, H. (2003). societal attachments, offending frequency, and techniques of neutralization. *Deviant Behavior,* 24(2), 101–127. http://doi.org/10.1080/01639620390117200

Cosmides, L., & Tooby, J. (2005). Social exchange: The evolutionary design of a neurocognitive system. Hämtad från http://citeseerx.ist.psu.edu/viewdoc/summary?doi=10.1.1.140.5888

Daly, K. (1989). Gender and Varieties of White-Collar Crime*. *Criminology,* 27(4), 769–794. http://doi.org/10.1111/j.1745-9125.1989.tb01054.x

Dean, D. H. (2004). Perceptions of the Ethicality of Consumer Insurance Claim Fraud. *Journal of Business Ethics,* 54(1), 67–79. http://doi.org/10.1023/B:BUSI.0000043493.79787.e6

DeLisi, M., & Piquero, A. R. (2011). New frontiers in criminal careers research, 2000–2011: A state-of-the-art review. *Journal of Criminal Justice,* 39(4), 289–301. http://doi.org/10.1016/j.jcrimjus.2011.05.001

Ellis, L., & Walsh, A. (1997). Gene-Based Evolutionary Theories in Criminology*. *Criminology,* 35(2), 229–276. http://doi.org/10.1111/j.1745-9125.1997.tb00876.x

Farrington, D. P. (2003). Developmental and Life-Course Criminology: Key Theoretical And Empirical Issues-The 2002 Sutherland Award Address*. *Criminology,* 41(2), 221–225. http://doi.org/10.1111/j.1745-9125.2003.tb00987.x

Farrington, D. P. (2008). Integrated Developmental and Life-Course Theories of Offending (Advances in Criminological Theory). *Transaction Publishers.*

Feeley, D. (2006). Personality, Environment, and the Causes of White-Collar Crime. *Law & Psychology Review,* 30, 201.

Gottschalk, P. (2013). Empirical Differences in Crime Categories by White-Collar Criminals. International Letters of Social and Humanistic Sciences, (05), 17–26.

Haantz, S. (2002). Women and White Collar Crime. National White Collar Crime Center http://www. nw3c. org/downloads/women_wcc1. pdf. Hämtad från http://www.jpsimsconsulting.com/site_media/cms_page_media/44/Women%20and%20White-Collar-Crime.pdf

Hamilton, W. D. (1964). The genetical evolution of social behaviour. I. *Journal of Theoretical Biology,* 7(1), 1–16. http://doi.org/10.1016/0022-5193(64)90038-4

Holtfreter, K., Beaver, K. M., Reisig, M. D., & Pratt, T. C. (2010). Low self-control and fraud offending. *Journal of Financial Crime,* 17(3), 295–307. http://doi.org/10.1108/13590791011056264

Holtfreter, K., Van Slyke, S., & Blomberg, T. G. (2005). Sociolegal change in consumer fraud: From victim-offender interactions to global networks. *Crime, Law and Social Change,* 44(3), 251–275.

Jacobsson, K. (2011). Accounts of Honesty: Refuting Allegations of Bribery. *Deviant Behavior,* 33(2), 108–125. http://doi.org/10.1080/01639625.2010.548294

Kardell, J., & Bergqvist, M. (2009). Equal Treatment in Swedish Economic Crime Investigations: Do Professional Specialization and the Suspect's Social Background Matter? *Journal of Scandinavian Studies in Criminology and Crime Prevention,* 10(2), 76–101. http://doi.org/10.1080/14043850903320396

Kerley, K. R., & Copes, H. (2004). The Effects of Criminal Justice Contact on Employment Stability for White-Collar and Street-Level Offenders. *International Journal of Offender Therapy and Comparative Criminology,* 48(1), 65 –84. http://doi.org/10.1177/0306624X03256660

Klenowski, P. M., Copes, H., & Mullins, C. W. (2010). Gender, Identity, and Accounts: How White Collar Offenders Do Gender When Making Sense of Their Crimes. *Justice Quarterly,* 28(1), 46–69. http://doi.org/10.1080/07418825.2010.482536

Krohn, M. D., Gibson, C. L., & Thornberry, T. P. (2013). Under the Protective Bud the Bloom Awaits: A Review of Theory and Research on Adult-Onset and Late-Blooming Offenders. I C. L. Gibson & M. D. Krohn (Reds), Handbook of Life-Course Criminology (ss 183–200). *Springer* New York. Hämtad från http://link.springer.com/chapter/10.1007/978-1-4614-5113-6_11

Larsson, D. (2013). The Reaction Towards White Collar Crime: When White Collar Crime Matters. *The Open Criminology Journal,* 6(1), 1–9. http://doi.org/10.2174/1874917801306010001

Laub, J. H., & Sampson, R. J. (2003). Shared beginnings, divergent lives : delinquent boys to age 70. Cambridge, MA: *Harvard University Press.*

Listwan, S. J., Piquero, N. L., & Van Voorhis, P. (2010). Recidivism Among a White-Collar Sample: Does Personality Matter? *Australian and New Zealand Journal of Criminology,* 43(1), 156–174. http://doi.org/10.1375/acri.43.1.156

Mangels, N. J. (2000). Latent biases in biocriminological research. *The Justice Professional,* 13(2), 105–123. http://doi.org/10.1080/1478601X.2000.9959579

McGuire, J. (2004). Understanding psychology and crime: perspectives on theory and action. *McGraw-Hill International.*

Mealey, L. (1995). The sociobiology of sociopathy: An integrated evolutionary model. *Behavioral and Brain Sciences, 18*(Special Issue 03), 523–541. http://doi.org/10.1017/S0140525X00039595

Menard, S., & Morris, R. (2012). Integrated Theory and Crimes of Trust. *Journal of Quantitative Criminology,* 28(2), 365–387. http://doi.org/10.1007/s10940-011-9142-x

Minor, W. W. (1981). Techniques of Neutralization: A Reconceptualization and Empirical Examination. *Journal of Research in Crime and Delinquency,* 18(2), 295–318. http://doi.org/10.1177/002242788 101800 206

Onna, J. H. R. van, Geest, V. R. van der, Huisman, W., & Denkers, A. J. M. (2014). Criminal Trajectories of White-collar Offenders. *Journal of Research in Crime and Delinquency,* 0022427814531489. http://doi.org /10.1177/0022427814531489

Piquero, A. R., Farrington, D. P., & Blumstein, A. (2007). Key issues in criminal career research : new analyses of the Cambridge Study in Delinquent Development. New York: *Cambridge University Press.* Hämtad från http://www.loc.gov/catdir/enhancements/fy0642/20060 11725-d.html

Piquero, N. L., & Benson, M. L. (2004). White-Collar Crime and Criminal Careers. *Journal of Contemporary Criminal Justice,* 20(2), 148 –165. http://doi.org/10.1177/1043986204263770

Poortinga, E., Lemmen, C., & Jibson, M. D. (2006). A Case Control Study: White-Collar Defendants Compared With Defendants Charged With Other Nonviolent Theft. *J Am Acad Psychiatry Law,* 34(1), 82–89.

Raine, A., Laufer, W. S., Yang, Y., Narr, K. L., Thompson, P., & Toga, A. W. (nd). Increased executive functioning, attention, and cortical thickness in white-collar criminals. *Human Brain Mapping.* http://doi.org/10.1002 /hbm.21415

Rosenfeld, R., & Messner, S. F. (2013). *Crime and the Economy. SAGE.*

Rothman, M. L., & Gandossy, R. P. (1982). Sad Tales: The Accounts of White-Collar Defendants and the Decision to Sanction. *The Pacific Sociological Review,* 25(4), 449–473.

Rutter, M. (2010). Gene–environment interplay. *Depression and Anxiety,* 27(1), 1–4. http://doi.org/10.1002/da.20641

Scott-Phillips, T. C., Dickins, T. E., & West, S. A. (2011). Evolutionary Theory and the Ultimate–Proximate Distinction in the Human Behavioral Sciences. *Perspectives on Psychological Science,* 6(1), 38–47. http://doi.org/10.1177/1745691610393528

Shaw, C. R., & McKay, H. D. (1969). Juvenile Delinquency and Urban Areas. Hämtad från http://www.eric.ed.gov/ERICWebPortal/detail?accno=ED036950

Shechory, M., Perry, G., & Addad, M. (2011). Pathways to Women's Crime: Differences Among Women Convicted of Drug, Violence and Fraud Offenses. *The Journal of Social Psychology,* 151(4), 399–416. http://doi.org/10.1080/00224545.2010.503721

Shover, N., Coffey, G. S., & Hobbs, D. (2003). Crime on the Line. Telemarketing and the Changing Nature of Professional Crime. *British Journal of Criminology,* 43(3), 489–505. http://doi.org/10.1093/bjc/43.3.489

Shover, N., & Hochstetler, A. (2005). Choosing White-Collar Crime. *Cambridge University Press.*

Shover, N., Hochstetler, A., & Alalehto, T. (2012). Choosing White-Collar Crime. I F. T. Cullen & P. Wilcox (Reds), The Oxford Handbook of Criminological Theory. *Oxford University Press.* Hämtad från http://www.oxfordhandbooks.com/view/10.1093/oxfordhb/9780199747238.001.0001/oxfordhb-9780199747238-e-25#oxfordhb-9780199747238-div1-127

Simons, R. L., & Lei, M. K. (2013). Enhanced Susceptibility to Context: A Promising Perspective on the Interplay of Genes and the Social Environment. I C. L. Gibson & M. D. Krohn (Reds), Handbook of Life-Course Criminology (ss 57–67). *Springer New York.* Hämtad från http://link.springer.com/chapter/10.1007/978-1-4614-5113-6_4

Soothill, K., Humphreys, L., & Francis, B. (2012). Middle-Class Offenders A 35-Year Follow-Up. *British Journal of Criminology,* 52(4), 765–785. http://doi.org/10.1093/bjc/azs014

Sutherland, E. H. (1985). White Collar Crime: The Uncut Version. Y*ale University Press.*

Tabery, J. (2007). Biometric and developmental gene–environment interactions: *Looking back, moving forward. Development and Psychopathology,* 19(04), 961–976. http://doi.org/10.1017/S0954579407000478

Tittle, C. R. (1995). Control balance : toward a general theory of deviance. Boulder, Colo.: *Westview Press.*

Tittle, C. R. (2004). Refining control balance theory. *Theoretical Criminology,* 8(4), 395 –428. http://doi.org/10.1177/1362480604046657

Trivers, R. L. (1971). The Evolution of Reciprocal Altruism. *The Quarterly Review of Biology,* 46(1), 35–57.

Waal, F. de. (1996). Good natured : the origins of right and wrong in humans and other animals. Cambridge, MA.: *Harvard Univ. Press.*

Waal, F. de, & Redmalm, G. (2005). Vår inre apa : det bästa och sämsta i den mänskliga naturen. Stockholm: *Svenska förlaget.*

Walsh, A., & Beaver, K. M. (2009). Biosocial criminology. London: *Routledge.*

Walsh, A., & Ellis, L. (2003). Biosocial Criminology: Challenging Environmentalism's Supremacy. *Nova Science Publishers.*

Walsh, A., & Wu, H. (2008). Differentiating antisocial personality disorder, psychopathy, and sociopathy: evolutionary, genetic, neurological, and sociological considerations. *Criminal Justice Studies,* 21(2), 135–152. http://doi.org/10.1080/14786010802159814

Walters, G. D., & Geyer, M. D. (2004). Criminal Thinking and Identity in Male White-Collar Offenders. *Criminal Justice and Behavior,* 31(3), 263 –281. http://doi.org/10.1177/0093854803262508

Weisburd, D. (1991a). Crimes of the middle classes: White-collar offenders in the federal courts. *Yale Univ Pr.*

Weisburd, D. (1991b). Crimes of the middle classes: White-collar offenders in the federal courts. *Yale Univ Pr.*

Weisburd, D., Waring, E. J., & Chayet, E. (2001). White-collar crime and criminal careers. *Cambridge Univ Pr.*

West, S. A., El Mouden, C., & Gardner, A. (2011). Sixteen common misconceptions about the evolution of cooperation in humans. *Evolution and Human Behavior,* 32(4), 231–262. http://doi.org/10.1016/j.evolhumbehav.2010.08.001

Wheeler, S., Weisburd, D., Waring, E., & Bode, N. (1988). White Collar Crimes and Criminals. *American Criminal Law Review*, 25(3), 27.

Wiebe, R. P. (2012). Integrating Criminology Through Adaptive Strategy and Life History Theory. *Journal of Contemporary Criminal Justice,* 28(3), 346–365. http://doi.org/10.1177/1043986212450231

Wikström, P.-O. H., & Sampson, R. J. (2009). The explanation of crime : context, mechanisms and development. Cambridge: *Cambridge University Press.*

Wright, J. P., & Boisvert, D. (2009). What Biosocial Criminology Offers Criminology. *Criminal Justice and Behavior,* 36(11), 1228 –1240. http://doi.org/10.1177/0093854809343140

Wärneryd, K.-E., & Walerud, B. (1982). Taxes and economic behavior: Some interview data on tax evasion in Sweden. *Journal of Economic Psychology,* 2(3), 187–211. http://doi.org/10.1016/0167-4870(82)90003-4

Yao, S., Långström, N., Temrin, H., & Walum, H. (nd). Criminal offending as part of an alternative reproductive strategy: investigating evolutionary hypotheses using Swedish total population data. *Evolution and Human Behavior*. http://doi.org/10.1016/j.evolhumbehav.2014.06.007

In: Advances in Criminology Research
Editor: Julia Guzman ISBN: 978-1-63483-180-2

Chapter 3

CATEGORIZATION, STEREOTYPING, STATUS AND POLICE TRAFFIC STOP BEHAVIOR

***Christopher Barnum**[*,1], **Michael Lovaglia**[2] and **Jared Miller**[1]*
[1]St. Ambrose University, US
[2]The University of Iowa, US

INTRODUCTION

The social sciences have long been interested in the ways that an individual's demographic characteristics such as race, gender and age shape behavior in applied settings where people differ in power and status. In recent years this interest has been fueled by high profile news stories about mistreatment of segments of the population at the hands of powerful actors. Research on police bias for example, has found that minority members are often overrepresented in police-citizen encounters including stops and arrests (Alpert, MacDonald, & Dunham, 2005; Batton & Kadleck, 2004; Engel, Calnon & Bernard, 2002; McMahon, Garner, Davis & Kraus, 2002; Rice & White, 2010; Rojek, Rosenfeld & Decker, 2012; Withrow, 2006, but also see Blank, Dabady & Citro, 2004). These findings are consistent across a broad

[*] Send correspondence to: First author at: barnumchristopherc@sau.edu

range of research methodologies and wide variety of law enforcement agencies. While the overall conclusion from these studies is clear—the police to varying degrees tend to disproportionately stop or sanction minority members—the reasons for disproportionality are less evident. Recent theorizing has proffered a number of explanations for the sources of disparity. These include status differences between the police and minority members, police perceptions of criminal activity in an area, social psychological processes, implicit cognitive bias, econometric models as well as racial profiling and directed patrol (Batton & Kadleck, 2004; Black, 1976, 1980; Close & Mason, 2007; Correll, Park, Judd & Wittenbrink, 2002; Klinger, 1997; Payne, 2005; Rojek, Rosenfeld & Decker, 2012; Smith & Alpert, 2007; Smith, Makarios & Alpert, 2006).

In what follows we present a theory that describes the association between social categories and inequitable police enforcement behavior. Our model builds upon previous work by explicitly linking ideas from several key areas of investigation including: status characteristics theory from sociology (Berger, Cohen & Zelditch, 1972; Berger, Norman, Balkwell, & Smith, 1992; Ridgeway & Erickson, 2002); Black's theory of law (Black, 1976, 1980; Rojek, Rosenfeld & Decker, 2012); theories of implicit "shooter bias" from psychology (e. g., Correll et al., 2002; Greenwald, Oakes & Hoffman, 2003; Payne, 2001) and recent social psychological theorizing found in criminal justice (e. g., Novak & Chamlin, 2008; Smith & Alpert, 2007).

The new theory advances previous police disproportionality frameworks in an important way. The concept of status is operationalized more comprehensively than has been done before to include multiple status features salient in the context. For example, instead of ordering predictions for police intervention solely in terms of a single characteristic, like race, the theory explicitly uses multiple features to predict police enforcement behavior. Previous theoretical formulations have left some status characteristics like age and gender implicit. Our theory specifies these and predicts that distinct combinations of these characteristics are associated with perceptions of criminality and social rank that affect the application of law in police-citizen encounters. This claim builds in part on the *race out-of-place* hypothesis, which posits that the police disproportionately stop target-drivers whose race is incongruent with the surrounding neighborhood demographics (Novak & Chamlin, 2008; Rojek, Rosenfeld & Decker, 2012; Withrow, 2006). However, since our theory hypothesizes that enforcement behavior is shaped by *multiple* salient status characteristics and not just by race alone, it predicts that disproportionality results from police perceptions of several salient characteristics. Consequently, the police are not likely to disproportionately stop *all* drivers whose race is out-of-place in a neighborhood, but rather, will be more likely to stop the drivers they deem as most suspicious. Simply put, the police are more likely to be suspicious of specific combinations of status characteristics than of others. So for instance, we predict that the police will be less likely to disproportionately stop elderly black women than young black males in an all-white neighborhood even though the race of both types of drivers is out of place.

The following sections first briefly review the relevant literature on police bias. This is followed by a statement of our model and then several testable propositions. This chapter wraps up with a summary and conclusion.

Literature Review

Background

Racially biased policing which is sometimes called racial profiling has existed in various forms for generations in the United States. However, the practice became increasingly controversial in the 1980s when some of the first Drug Enforcement Administration sponsored programs came into existence. *Operation Pipeline*, for example, was a federal program developed to assist local law enforcement officials in the identification and interdiction of potential drug couriers. Initially, its tactics included using race as an indicator of suspiciousness. Such programs generated animosity among minority members that ultimately led to litigation. As a result many agencies across America began collecting data on police-citizen contacts. Several studies have used portions of these data to investigate disproportionality in police traffic stop activity. In general, these studies have found that police more frequently stop, search, and sanction minority drivers than nonminority drivers (for reviews see Batton & Kadleck, 2004; Engel, Calnon & Bernard, 2002; McMahon, Garner, Davis & Kraus 2002; Withrow, 2006).

Some researchers suggest that racially biased policing can be grouped into four “ideal types” (Weber, 1958) and that at least one of these four processes is likely to be present in any context where unjustified racial disparity is occurring in traffic stops (Batton & Kadleck, 2004; Novak, 2004; Novak & Chamlin, 2008; Smith, Makarios & Alpert 2006). These processes include *discrimination*, *unconscious cognitive activity*, *racial profiling* and *directed patrol*. The first two of these are a product of human agency and stem from social psychological processes. The other two sources are generated by social-structural norms and expectations. *Discrimination* is negative behavior directed towards others based on their membership in groups. *Unconscious cognitive bias* is automatic bias that requires no intentional decision making. *Racial profiling* refers to the explicit use of race as one trait in a set of identifiers employed by a law enforcement official to identify suspects. *Directed patrol* is a police deployment strategy that increases contact with minority citizens. In this chapter we focus on social psychological processes.

Black's Theory of Law

Black's theory of law (1976, 1980) is a systematic formulation that generates testable predictions about the settings in which the law is applied. The chief claim of the theory is that a person's relative social position or status is the principal factor in determining whether the law will be invoked in a given enforcement context. The theory conceptualizes social status using personal demographic indicators such as differences in wealth, organization and culture (Rojek, Rosenfeld & Decker, 2012).

When applied to police behavior, Black's theory argues that the decision of the police to take action is partly determined by the relative social status of officers and their targets. The theory assumes a downward application of the law. Consequently, an officer's decision to stop, detain, search or arrest a target-person is a function of the relative social status between an officer and their target. The theory also assumes that individuals with relative higher status are more likely to invoke the law than are individuals possessing relative lower status. Empirical tests of Black's theory have generally framed status solely in terms of race. This leads to the following ordering in the likelihood of the application of the law in police-citizen encounters: (1) white officer-minority citizen (2) white officer-white citizen, (3) black officer-black citizen and (4) black officer-white citizen. A recent study has found support for this ordering in police searches (Rojek, Rosenfeld & Decker, 2012).

Status Characteristics Theory

Status characteristics theory suggests ways in which expectations about individuals shape the decisions and behavior in work settings, including police work. Status characteristics research investigates how socially valued traits of individuals alter the respect that people have for each other. In contemporary American society *diffuse status characteristics* such as a person's race, gender and age produce expectations for that person's social value and moral worth (Berger, Wagner & Zelditch, 1985). Most research using the theory has been in small work groups where members with highly valued characteristics gain influence over group decisions. The status characteristics and expectation states research program is notable for developing theory that makes precise numerical predictions that can be tested using a variety of empirical observation methods. The theory has also contributed to research on teaching in heterogeneous classrooms, standardized testing, and the prestige of organizations (Cohen & Lotan, 1995; Lovaglia, Lucas, Houser, Thye & Markovsky, 1998; Podolny, 1993).

Status characteristics theory proposes that members who possess higher states of status characteristics are expected to be more competent and thus more valuable than those possessing lower states, men more than women, whites more than blacks. Such expectation states are non-conscious and can co-exist with an individual's firmly held belief in social equality. The theory explains how these performance expectations lead to the emergence of differentiated power, prestige and influence structures among task group members. Relative to lower status members, higher status members are thereby advantaged with respect to the group's *observable power and prestige order*. A series of related assumptions lays out the theory's causal sequence culminating in a prediction of overall expectation (dis)advantage based on the combined impact of an individual's various status characteristics salient in the situation (Wagner & Berger, 2006). For example, the theory gives precise numerical predictions for the degree of expectation disadvantage experienced by a 20 year-old black woman compared to a 35 year- old white man or between two individuals with any combination of salient status characteristics. Interestingly, status characteristics theory's explanation for why a given trait becomes a status characteristic rather than remaining a mere descriptor employs a causal mechanism similar to that used by Smith and Alpert (2007) to explain police bias.

Smith and Alpert's Theory

Smith and Alpert's (2007) theory attempts a complete social psychologically oriented explanation of police bias from a criminal justice perspective. The theory proposes that individual-level police conduct is guided by unconscious biases toward minority citizens. This bias forms through one of two processes involving implicit schemas and stereotypes: *(i)* those that develop from repeated differential exposure to criminality involving minority groups and *(ii)* those formed through illusory correlation, negative impressions formed when interacting with a member of a numerical minority. The theory assumes that the salience of racially biased policing in the public consciousness makes it improbable that alternative explanations based on explicit racism or the strategic use of race account for the racial disparity found in studies. Instead, Smith and Alpert propose that implicit cognitive activity, such as automatic schema formation and stereotyping, is a more probable source of disparity. These constructs become activated from familiar environmental cues and because they are implicit, resist detection during job screening and assessment. The theory proposes that even police officers that begin their careers without racial bias tend to acquire expectations of increased criminality for some classifications of minorities.

Smith and Alpert (2007) propose that non-volitional processes generate significant proportions of the disparity observed in empirical data from studies of police traffic enforcement activity, primarily unconscious stereotyping mechanisms. Stereotypes most important for explaining police bias are those formed through internalization of important personal experiences stemming from repeated exposure. Significantly, these stereotypes originate from the nature of police work itself, where police are in daily contact with people likely to be both criminals and members of minority groups. The theory proposes that negative stimuli make a stronger impression than positive stimuli. Because police officers are repeatedly exposed to negative environmental stimuli while dealing disproportionately with members of minority groups, police officers develop unconscious bias toward them.

Illusory correlation is Smith and Alpert's (2007) second major theoretical element. Illusory correlation has been found to occur in laboratory settings where people arbitrarily placed in a numerical minority group are rated more negatively than people placed in a numerical majority group (Hamilton & Gifford, 1976; Hamilton, Dugan & Trolier, 1985). Studies to date find the illusory correlation effect to be robust, moderate in size, and highly significant (McConnell, Sherman & Hamilton 1994; Mullen & Johnson, 1990). Smith and Alpert propose that in certain contexts negative stimuli inevitable in police work are disproportionately associated in officers' minds with specific minority groups creating an illusory correlation between a suspect's race or gender and that suspect's dangerousness. A different interpretation of the impact of illusory correlation on police bias is perhaps more likely. Novak and

Chamlin (2008) propose that police suspicion increases when observing a member of a numerical minority, for example a white driver in a black neighborhood. They found that in majority black areas, police searched white motorists at a higher rate than they did in majority white areas.

Experimental Research Investigating Weapons and Shooter Bias

Recent research in psychology explores a phenomenon known as weapon or shooter bias, the consistent laboratory finding that race affects participants' decisions about the meaning of targets in contexts requiring snap judgments. This tradition uses laboratory experiments that simulate one of two settings. In the first, participants perform a laboratory task where they either attempt to distinguish a weapon from a harmless object (after being primed by race), while in the second setting, they decide whether to "shoot" or "not shoot" a selection of virtual human targets that vary by race (Correll et al., 2002; Greenwald et al., 2003; Payne, 2001). In both settings race is irrelevant to the task. However, results consistently indicate that participants rely on race in making decisions. To explain this finding, researchers use a *two processes* model that integrates intentional and unintentional aspects of behavior to explain this finding (Payne, 2005, 2006; Payne, Lambert, & Jacoby 2002). Unintentional behavior is an automatic cognitive response to a stereotype that occurs without any purposeful cognitive functioning (Lepore & Brown, 2002). Unintentional automatic cognitive activity interacts with purposeful intentions such that, although racial animus is sufficient to produce bias, it is not necessary. Thus, bias can coexist with fair-minded intentions. This work demonstrates that automatic stereotypes regularly affect behavioral decisions in circumstances where people are rushed, under pressure, or distracted. These are conditions that typify police work. Because police bias remains a problem despite training designed to remove it, we focus on unintentional and unconscious processes to explain it.

In the wake of the 1999 police shooting where four police officers fired 41 shots killing an unarmed black man named Amadou Diallo, researchers proposed that race becomes a salient indicator of a suspect's *dangerousness* for police officers in threatening situations (Correll, Park, Judd, & Wittenbrink, 2002). Using a video simulation where participants made repeated decisions to shoot or not shoot black and white men that were either armed or unarmed, participants more quickly decided to shoot unarmed black targets and to not shoot armed white targets. The bias toward shooting black targets occurred for both black and white shooters. This result implies that in-group/out-group explanations for racial stereotypes are inadequate for explaining bias in police shootings. Recent studies have found that participants shoot both black and white targets more readily in threatening situations but that they are biased toward shooting black targets in non-threatening situations (Correll, Wittenbrink, Park, Judd, & Goyle, 2011).

More recently, James, Klinger and Vila (2014) investigated shooter bias using a realistic HD video simulated model and citizens as subject-participants. This design presented participants with ultra-realistic, filmed interactive scenarios like those used for police training. These scenarios depicted various scenes common in law enforcement such as traffic stops, alarms and domestic disturbances. Instead of the hand-held button used in the psychological studies outlined above, the participants here used modified semi-automatic handguns with gun-barrels fitted with laser-emitters that registered shot placement on the screen. As before, in some of these scenarios suspects were depicted as carrying deadly weapons, while in others, the targets were holding innocuous items. Researchers also fitted participants with EEG caps and recorded their brain-wave activity. The dependent variables for this study included *(i)* EEG responses, *(ii)* incorrect weapon-responses when firing at a target and *(iii)* the amount of time to shoot.

Results from this experiment show that contrary to previous findings, subjects' behavior was actually *less* biased against minority targets than white targets. Although brain wave activity suggested that subjects exhibited implicit cognitive bias and threat responses towards black targets, but not white targets, subjects actually took longer to shoot armed black targets than armed white targets. The authors reason that this response may be due to a "behavioral counter bias" that is rooted in concerns about the consequences of shooting a historically oppressed minority member (James, Klinger & Vila, 2014).

A Theory of Police Expectations

The foregoing theories explain how social structure generates cognitive or emotional reactions with important consequences for individuals, relationships and groups. We use ideas from these works to complete our model predicting aspects of police behavior. Our theory starts from the perspective of a single police officer. The theory requires that this actor be oriented toward other actors in the setting, *targets*. Each of the targets is defined by one or more traits called *status characteristics*. These traits include demographic features such as race, age and gender. Each trait has a finite number of levels each associated with connotations of social worth, which means that most people in a society consider it better to be one state than another. The officer makes decisions concerning the targets and desires to make correct decisions. Such decisions center on the officer's expectation of the targets' *likelihood for criminality*, and overall *social status*. We also assume that the targets are strangers to the officer and interaction between the officer and the target-person is dyadic. Finally we assume that nothing else defines the setting.

Description of the Model

Our theory proposes that under circumstances within its scope, demands generated by an enforcement context cause certain personal traits or status characteristics to become salient. The various levels of these traits activate expectations that are relevant for behavior. This process occurs automatically and implicitly. No animus on the part of police officers is assumed. All else being equal, the traits that become salient are those that differentiate targets. For simplicity in making initial predictions, our model focuses on demographic characteristics highly salient to police officers—gender, race, and age. These are characteristics typically used by witnesses to describe a perpetrator. "He was white, mid-twenties." Additional characteristics can be added later to refine the model.

Each salient status characteristic is associated with a specific value on *two* theoretical dimensions important to the police when deciding whether to stop or apprehend a target. First and most important is the *likelihood for criminality*, the automatic expectation about the potential for a target-person to break the law. Most officers view their role primarily in terms of protecting others and fighting crime. "Police officers see themselves first and foremost as crime fighters—soldiers in a war on crime with battle lines drawn between [the police] and [criminals]" (Smith and Alpert, 2007 p. 1276). Consequently, to make effective use of their time, officers want to focus their interactions with the public on those individuals most likely to have committed a chargeable offense. The idea of dangerousness is subsumed under this theoretical dimension. All else being equal, an officer who perceives another as dangerous, is also likely to perceive the person as somebody who is willing to engage in criminal conduct.

Various classifications of race, age and gender are associated with specific perceptions for criminality. For instance, previous research has demonstrated that many people perceive certain categories as more "criminal" than others (LaGrange & Ferraro, 1989). This perception frequently stems from media accounts and often centers on young people, males and African-Americans (Chiricos, Eschholz & Gertz, 1997; Hurwitz & Peffley, 1997; LaGrange & Ferraro, 1989; Oliver & Fonash, 2002; Peffley & Hurwitz, 1992; Romer, Hall-Jamieson & Aday, 2003; Russell, 1995; Steffensmeier, Ulmer & Kramer, 1998; Williams & Dickinson, 1993). Ideas about expectations for criminality form the core of our first theoretical claims:

(1) For police officers, specific states of a target-person's salient status characteristics (e. g., age, gender and race) generate implicit and automatic cognitive expectations about the likelihood that the person will break the law.
    (a) Expectations from each salient characteristic combine
    (b) These expectations affect enforcement behavior.

The second theoretical dimension important to police officers deciding whether to stop or apprehend a target is the expected *social status* of the person. Expectations for a person's social status can be estimated from observable status characteristics salient in the situation (Berger, Wagner, & Zelditch, 1985). As noted, our theory focuses on three characteristics, gender, race, and age. Social status can impact an officer's assessment in two ways: High social status indicates (a) the target-person has high commitment to approved social values thus may be less likely to offend, and (b) the individual possesses resources and influence to counter a criminal charge, increasing risk to the officer. Moreover, following Black (1976, 1980) we assume that the police utilize a downward application of the law and consequently in dyadic encounters, the police are more likely to invoke enforcement against citizens with lower relative social status than against those with higher relative status.

Researchers have typically utilized race as an indicator of social status in enforcement contexts. For instance, Rojek, Rosenfeld and Decker (2012) argue that race predicts the application of the law in contexts where officers are searching motorists. Our theory posits that other features of the setting, including age and gender, also induce expectations for status and therefore affect police enforcement behavior. Consequently, we argue it is necessary to simultaneously examine the impact of multiple salient status characteristics in enforcement contexts. Simply put, when evaluating predictions about the application of law in police-citizen encounters, instead of ordering predictions solely in terms of a single characteristic—like race—multiple salient status characteristics should be included in theoretical models. This leads to the following claims:

(2) For police officers, specific states of target-person's salient status characteristics (e. g., age, gender and race) generate implicit and automatic cognitive expectations about the individual's social status.
   (a) Expectations from each characteristic combine
   (b) These expectations affect enforcement behavior.
   (c) Enforcement behavior is characterized by a downward application of the law in terms of relative status.

The model assumes that expectations for status and the likelihood to offend are correlated rather than orthogonal. For instance, all else being equal, an officer is more likely to perceive a person who is lower in relative status as more likely to offend than a person who is of higher status. Although we assume that correlations between the dimensions are moderate, establishing the exact correlation is an empirical question for further research. An officer's decision to make contact with a subject can range in seriousness from stop/don't stop for a minor traffic violation all the way up to shoot/don't shoot in a violent encounter. We assume that criminality is given proportionally more weight in an officer's decision than is status, or:

(3) Although expectations about criminality and status combine, an officer's enforcement behavior is influenced more by expectations for criminality than by expectations for social status

The setting or context also impacts police enforcement activity. Prior research has demonstrated that rundown or dilapidated surroundings trigger perceptions of danger (Correll et al., 2011). It is also known that officers on patrol come to understand normal levels of crime in their areas and tend to respond with increased vigor to crimes they consider abnormal or deviant (Klinger, 1997). The police also perceive targets that seem incongruent or out of place in the setting as more suspicious than others (Novak & Chamlin, 2008; Rojek, Rosenfeld & Decker, 2012; Withrow, 2006). Since specific classifications of age, race and gender are linked with expectations for criminality, police enforcement activity can lead to minority bias and disproportionality. Interestingly however, research from the shooter bias paradigm in psychology has demonstrated that bias directed towards minority members by police officers tends to *decrease* in contexts that connote danger

(Correll et al., 2011). This body of work focuses on how race stimulates automatic stereotypes that affect people's snap judgments about the meaning of ambiguous targets. An important finding from this tradition is that bias tends to decrease in contexts where people perceive increased danger or threat. Importantly, the perception of threat can be created by danger cues originating from either the environment or from characteristics of the target-person. These ideas are summarized in the following claim:

(4) The police perceive targets that seem incongruent or out of place in the setting as more suspicious than others and bias in police enforcement behavior *decreases* in social contexts that connote extreme danger.

To summarize, as the police patrol their beats, they encounter countless individuals, some of whom may be criminals. Officers must be able to quickly "size-up" or judge people in order to identify potential suspects. Our theory posits that for police officers, the target-person's age, gender and race generate automatic and implicit expectations about the likelihood for criminality and social status. In many cases, specific states of the target-person's demographic characteristics—including being young, or a minority member, or a male—are associated with increased expectations for criminality. As officers participate in enforcement activity, these expectations can result in bias and disproportionality in enforcement outcomes. Simply put, expectations associated with various demographic classifications of potential enforcement targets can function to increase levels of disparity in police enforcement behavior.

Concurrently with expectations for criminality, perceptions associated with the social status also affect enforcement behavior. As officers go about their duties, a target-person's age, gender and race generate automatic cognitive expectations regarding the person's social rank (Berger, Wagner, & Zelditch, 1985). In an enforcement encounter, suspects with increasing social status may suggest to the officer that these people are likely to hold the resources and influence necessary to counter a criminal charge if arrested. Given this, we argue that an officer is more likely to enforce the law against a potential suspect possessing lower relative social status than the officer. Finally, we assume that the context surrounding an enforcement encounter influences expectations. Contexts that signify significant danger decrease differences in expectations for criminality. As a result, bias and disproportionality decrease in these settings.

These ideas generate numerous theoretical derivations regarding which categories of people are likely to be disproportionately stopped and sanctioned by the police. For instance, given our present understanding of stereotypes and expectations for various demographic categories, the theory not only predicts that the levels of disproportionality in police traffic stop activity will be greater for young, black men than young, white men, but also that disproportionality will be greater for young white men than senior black women. The second claim is somewhat non-intuitive and follows from our theoretical argument that the impact of expectations for criminality and status combine across multiple salient status characteristics. The theory generates many other similar types of claims.

CONCLUSION

"Racial bias" is a blanket explanation for the empirical reality that African-American men tend to be over represented in data investigating police traffic stop, arrest, and shooting behavior. We propose a more nuanced model. Our approach is predicated on the assumption that multiple traits, like race, gender and age interact with important contextual information including an officer's understanding of a suspect's potential for criminality and relative social rank, to generate bias. Our work builds upon concepts found in psychological theories of shooter bias, social cognitive theorizing found in criminal justice and sociological group process explanations for status differences. The model predicts that bias is more likely for certain members within a racial category than others. For example, bias is more likely for men than women and for the young than the old. This distinction enables our model to make predictions regarding a variety of contexts not previously possible. For example, our model can test whether young white men are more likely to be mistakenly shot by the police than older black men, or whether black women are more likely to be arrested for shoplifting than white men. Previous explanations predicated on a simple racial bias explanation cannot investigate these types of distinctions. Moreover, our model makes predictions for bias in a wide variety of police-citizen contexts ranging from shootings to traffic stops. If predictions from our model hold up under empirical testing, the theory can be applied to the development of intervention strategies to be used in the field with police officers.

REFERENCES

Alpert, G. P., Macdonald, J. M., & Dunham, R. G. (2005). Police suspicion and discretionary decision making during citizen stops. *Criminology,* 43(2), 407-434.

Batton, C., & Kadleck, C. (2004). Theoretical and methodological issues in racial profiling research. *Police Quarterly* 7, 30-64.

Berger, J., Cohen, B. P., & Zelditch, M. Jr. (1972). Status characteristics and social interaction. *American Sociological Review,* 37(3), 241-255.

Berger, J., Norman, R. Z., Balkwell, J., & Smith, R. F. (1992). Status inconsistency in task situations: A test of four status processing principles. *American Sociological Review,* 57, 843-855

Berger, J., Wagner, D., & Zelditch, M. Jr. (1985). Introduction: Expectation states theory: Review and assessment. Pp. 1 – 72.

Black, D. J. (1976). *The behavior of law.* New York: Academic Press. Pp. 1-203.

Black, D. J. (1980). *The manners and customs of the police.* New York: Academic Press. Pp. 1-274.

Blank, R. M., Dabady, M., & Citro, C. F. (2004). *Measuring racial discrimination.* National Research Council (Ed). Washington, DC: National Academies Press. Pp. 1-340.

Chiricos, T., Eschholz, S., & Gertz, M. (1997). Crime, news and fear of crime: Toward an identification of audience effects. *Social Problems* 44(3), 342-357.

Close, B., & Mason, P. (2007). Searching for efficient enforcement: Officer characteristics and racial biased policing. *Review of Law and Economics* 3, 263–321.

Cohen, E. G., & Lotan, R. A. (1995). Producing equal-status interaction in the heterogeneous classroom. *American Educational Research Journal* 32, 99-120.

Correll, J., Park, B., Judd, C. M., & Wittenbrink, B. (2002). The police officer's dilemma: Using ethnicity to disambiguate potentially threatening individuals. *Journal of Personality and Social Psychology.* 83, 1314-1329.

Correll, J., Wittenbrink, B., Park, B., Judd, C. M., & Goyle, A. (2011). Dangerous enough: Moderating racial bias with secondary threat cues. *Journal of Experimental Social Psychology,* 47, 184–189.

Engel, R. S., Calnon, J. M, & Bernard, T. J. (2002). Theory and racial profiling: Shortcomings and future directions in research. *Justice Quarterly* 19, 249-273.

Greenwald, A. G., Oakes, M. A., & Hoffman, H. G. (2003). Targets of discrimination: Effects of race on responses to weapons holders. *Journal of Experimental Psychology, 39*, 399–405.

Hamilton, D. L., & Gifford, R. K. (1976). Illusory correlation in interpersonal perception: A cognitive basis of stereotyping judgments. *Journal of Experimental Social Psychology.* 12, 392 – 407.

Hamilton, D. L., Dugan, P. M., & Trolier, T. K. (1985). The formation of stereotypic beliefs: Further evidence for distinctiveness-based illusory correlations. *Journal of Personality and Social Psychology*, 48, 5-17.

Hurwitz, J., & Peffley, M. (1997). Public perceptions of race and crime: The role of racial stereotypes. *American Journal of Political Science*, 41, 375-401.

James, L., Klinger, D., & Vila, B. (2014). Racial and ethnic bias in decisions to shoot seen through a stronger lens: Experimental results from high-fidelity laboratory simulations. *Journal of Experimental Criminology.* 10, 323-340.

Klinger, D. A. (1997). Negotiating order in patrol work: An ecological theory of police response to deviance. Criminology 35(2), 277-306.

LaGrange, R. L., & Ferraro, K. F. (1989). Assessing age and gender differences in perceived risk and fear of crime. *Criminology.* 27(4), 697-720.

Lepore, L., & Brown, R. (2002). The role of awareness: Divergent automatic stereotype activation and implicit judgment correction. *Social Cognition* 20, 321-351.

Lovaglia, M., Lucas, J., Houser, J., A., Thye, S., R., & Markovsky, B. (1998). Status processes and mental ability test scores. *American Journal of Sociology.* 104, 195-228.

McConnell, A. R., Sherman S.J., & Hamilton, D. L. (1994). Illusory correlation in the perception of groups: An extension of the distinctiveness-based account. *Journal of Personality and Social Psychology* 67, 414-429.

McMahon, J., Garner, J., Davis, R., & Kraus, A. (2002). How to correctly collect and analyze racial profiling data: Your reputation depends on it! Washington, DC: Department of Justice, Office of Community Oriented Policing Services, National Institute of Justice.

Mullen, B., & Johnson, C. (1990). *The Psychology of Consumer Behavior* Erlbaum Publishers. New Jersey.

Novak, K. (2004). Disparity and racial profiling in traffic enforcement. *Police Quarterly*, 7, 65-96.

Novak, K., & Chamlin, M. (2008). Racial threat, suspicion, and police behavior: The impact of race and place in traffic enforcement. *Crime & Delinquency, 58*(2), 275-300.

Oliver, M. B., & Fonash, D. (2002). Race and crime in the news: Whites' identification and misidentification of violent and nonviolent criminal suspects. *Media Psychology,* 4, 137-156.

Payne, B. K. (2001). Prejudice and perception: The role of automatic and controlled processes in misperceiving a weapon. *Journal of Personality and Social Psychology, 81*, 181–192.

Payne, B.K. (2005). Conceptualizing control in social cognition: How executive functioning modulates the expression of automatic stereotyping. *Journal of Personality and Social Psychology*, 89, 488–503.

Payne, B. K. (2006). Weapon bias: Split second decisions and unintended stereotyping. *Current Directions in Psychological Science.* 15, 287-291.

Payne, B. K., Lambert, A. J., & Jacoby, L. L. (2002). Best laid plans: Effects of goals on accessibility bias and cognitive control in race- based misperceptions of weapons. *Journal of Experimental Social Psychology, 38*, 384–396.

Peffley, M., & Hurwitz, J. (1992). Traditional versus social values as antecedents of racial stereotyping and policy conservatism. *Political Behavior*, 14(4), 395-421.

Podolny, J., M. (1993). A status-based model of market competition. *American Journal of Sociology* 98, 829-872.

Rice, S., & White, M. (2010). Race, ethnicity, and policing: New and essential readings. New York: New York University Press.

Ridgeway, C., & Erickson, K. (2002). Social status; Social perception: Social constructionism; Social interaction. *American Journal of Sociology.* 106, 579-615.

Rojek, J., Rosenfeld, R., & Decker, S. (2012). Policing race: The racial stratification of searches in police traffic stops. Criminology, 50(4), 993-1024.

Romer, D., Hall-Jamison, K., & Aday, S. (2003). Television news and the cultivation of fear of crime. *Journal of Communication,* 53(1), 88-104.

Russell, C. (1995). True Crime. *American Demographics*, 17(8), 22-31.

Smith, M. R., & Alpert G. P. (2007). A theory of social conditioning and illusory correlation. *Criminal Justice and Behavior* 34, 1262-1283.

Smith, M. R., Makarios, M., & Alpert, G. P. (2006). Differential suspicion: Theory specification and gender effects in the traffic stop context. *Justice Quarterly* 23, 271-295.

Steffensmeier, D., Ulmer, J., & Kramer, J. (1998). The interaction of race, gender, and age in criminal sentencing: The punishment cost of being young, black and male. Criminology, 36(4), 763-797.

Wagner, D., & Berger, J. (2006). Expectation states theory. In George Ritzer (Ed.), *The Blackwell Encyclopedia of Sociology.* Malden, MA: Blackwell Publishing.

Weber, M. (1958). *The Protestant ethic and the spirit of capitalism.* New York: Scribner.

Williams, P., & Dickinson, J. (1993). Fear of crime: Read all about it? The relationship between newspaper crime reporting and fear of crime. *British Journal of Criminology,* 33(1), 33-56.

Withrow, B. (2006). *Racial profiling: From rhetoric to reason.* New York: Prentice Hall.

In: Advances in Criminology Research
Editor: Julia Guzman
ISBN: 978-1-63483-180-2

Chapter 4

CAN DIFFERENCES IN ATTACHMENT TO PARENTS AND LEVEL OF SELF-CONTROL EXPLAIN THE GENDER GAP IN JUVENILE DELINQUENCY? TESTING A GENDERED ATTACHMENT–SELF-CONTROL THEORY

Helmut Hirtenlehner[1,*] and Brenda Sims Blackwell[2,1]
[1]Center for Criminology, Johannes Kepler University, Linz, Austria
[2]Department of Criminal Justice and Criminology, Georgia Southern University, Statesboro, GA, US

ABSTRACT

That boys are more likely to offend than girls is a well-established finding in contemporary criminology; however, few theoretical perspectives directly focus on explaining this gap. In 2002, Hayslett-McCall and Bernard introduced a new perspective, the gendered attachment–self-control theory, designed to explain the gender difference in criminal involvement. The theory posits that boys experience more

* Corresponding author: Helmut Hirtenlehner. Johannes Kepler University Linz, Center for Criminology, Altenberger Strasse 69, A – 4040 Linz, Austria. Tel: +49 732 2468 7446, e-mail: helmut.hirtenlehner@jku.at.
[1] Brenda Sims Blackwell: Department of Criminal Justice and Criminology, Georgia Southern University, Statesboro, GA. E-mail: bblackwell@georgiasouthern.edu.

disruptions in early attachments to primary caregivers, which leads to them developing less self-control and, consequently, a higher propensity to offend. This study assesses this perspective, which to date has been empirically neglected, using survey data from Austria. With boys reporting more crime and lower levels of both self-control and attachment to the mother than girls, and strong attachment to the mother being linked to weak self-control as well as low self-control predicting criminal behavior, the results provide some support for the theory.

Keywords: Gender, crime, attachment theory, self-control theory

INTRODUCTION

Gender is a key predictor of offending. Research repeatedly demonstrates that the prevalence and frequency of criminal behavior is higher for men than for women. Empirical evidence further suggests that the gender gap widens with the seriousness of the offense and that it is greater in official crime statistics than in self-report studies (Hirtenlehner et al., 2014a; Junger-Tas et al., 2004; Moffitt et al., 2001; Steffensmeier and Allan, 1996). It also is noted that the gender divide in criminal conduct is established early and tends to persist throughout lifecourse (Gottfredson and Hirschi 1990).

Theorizing about the relationship between gender and delinquency typically occurs within the frameworks of general theories of crime. In other words, attempts to explain why males commit more crime than females frequently draw from traditional criminological perspectives.

Theories explicitly focusing on the gendered nature of criminal behavior are rare (e.g. Hagan et al., 1987; Heimer and Matsueda, 1994; Messerschmidt, 1993; Steffensmeier and Allan, 1996)[1]. This remains true even amid the recent plethora of research generated in the past two decades that examines female, as well as male, criminality. One recent approach designed to address the gender gap in offending – and one that has not yet received direct empirical scrutiny – is Hayslett-McCall and Bernard's gendered attachment–self-control theory (2002). The theory basically posits that, due to culturally underpinned gendered child-rearing practices, boys experience more disruptions in early attachments to primary caregivers.

[1] Critical reflections on the linkages between a patriarchal society, gendered power differences and the gender ratio in criminal behavior are, of course, offered by feminist criminologists (Iovanni and Miller, 2008).

These disruptions then lead boys to develop less self-control and, consequently, a higher delinquent/criminal propensity. The perspective offered, while similar in many ways to earlier control theories, elaborates the construct of attachment by drawing on developmental psychology and writings on masculinities and crime, and utilizes the refined concept to specifically address the gender-crime gap.

The purpose of this article is to examine Hayslett-McCall and Bernard's gendered attachment–self-control theory by empirically testing core propositions of the explanatory model. Using data from a large-scale student survey conducted in Austria, this research specifically explores whether the gender gradient of juvenile delinquency reflects gendered differences in children's attachment to mothers and fathers, as well as associated self-control differentials between the sexes.

THEORY AND RESEARCH

While research on women, girls and crime has significantly grown in the past 30 years, largely represented through applications of traditional theories to either understand female criminality or explore sources of gender disparities in offending, theoretical development focused specifically on examining gender differences in crime has not kept pace. Indeed, only a few specific theoretical models have been offered as explanations of the gender gap in crime and delinquency, including power-control theory (Hagan et al., 1985), Heimer and Matsueda's theory of differential control (1994), and more recently, Hayslett-McCall and Bernard's gendered attachment–self-control theory (2002). While power-control theory has received substantial attention (Blackwell, 2000; Hirtenlehner et al., 2014a), Heimer and Matsueda's (1994) perspective has received less scrutiny, and, to date, the model offered by Hayslett-McCall and Bernard (2002) has not been tested at all. This is a notable absence, given the general lack of theoretical attention paid to the gender difference in criminal propensity and the inclusion of constructs in the gendered attachment–self control perspective that have been identified as salient for understanding this gap.

Each of these theories developed to specifically address the gender divide in crime and delinquency focuses on the key role played by socialization and control. However, the models highlight different processes through which gender differences in socialization experiences yield behavioral differences that reflect gendered expectations.

For example, power-control theory emphasizes the role played by parents, particularly mothers, in the amount and quality of supervision experienced by daughters compared to sons, linking these differences to risk preferences and risk perceptions, and, ultimately, crime. Meanwhile, Heimer (1996) highlights the importance of perceived social expectations for boys and girls and how parental controls and attachments impact the gendered development of these perceived expectations. Finally, Hayslett-McCall and Bernard (2002) focus on the role of parental attachment more directly, positing that boys, more than girls, are likely to experience a fracture of attachment to parents at a young age, largely through gendered child-rearing practices that are embedded in culturally normative beliefs about how boys and girls are to be raised. This model then explains that gender differences in self-control are a product of gender differences in early attachment to primary caregivers (mostly the mother). Ironically, given the plethora of studies on the role of low self-control in crime causation and the increasing focus on gender and crime, this latter model has stimulated no empirical research to date. The present paper seeks to address this vacancy.

Gendered Attachment–Self-Control Theory

As with other versions of control theory, the focus of Hayslett-McCall and Bernard's (2002) gendered attachment–self-control theory is on the role played by early socialization agents, primarily parents (in particular the mother). Consistent with Hirschi's (1969) social bonding theory, Gottfredson and Hirschi's (1990) general theory of crime, and Hagan et al.'s (1985) power-control theory, Hayslett-McCall and Bernard concentrate on attachment, chiefly to parents, and how this attachment facilitates the development of proclivities toward certain traits or tendencies that ultimately are linked to delinquency. In contrast to these other perspectives, which focus primarily on the amount of supervision, gendered attachment–self-control theory posits that parental supervision efforts generally vary in "kind" for boys and girls, and that these differences produce gendered differences in attachment that reflect cultural norms for masculinity and femininity. These gendered norms, according to Hayslett-McCall and Bernard, reflect an expectation that girls should maintain strong relationships, particularly with their parents, throughout the lifecourse, while boys should become independent and more individualistic, traits associated with masculinity (see e.g. Gilligan, 1982).

In developing their perspective, Hayslett-McCall and Bernard (2002) outline the importance of attachment drawing from developmental psychology. Specifically, they reference works of Bowlby (1969; 1988) and Ainsworth (1972), which assume that attachment is an innate need and that infants have natural attachment predilections. Thus, according to these theorists attachment is a natural state, and rather it is detachment that is acquired. Individuals who experience reaffirmation of their attachment needs to significant others are likely to exhibit numerous prosocial outcomes throughout adolescence and adulthood.

Detachment, or damage to the secure attachment to significant others, is assumed by these same developmental psychologists to occur when, in stressful environments, children between 2-3 years of age experience parental separation, harsh, punitive parenting strategies, inconsistency in discipline, lack of assistance or neglect and rejection by their parents. Disruptions of this nature create insecure bonds to mothers and fathers (see also Gottfredson and Hirschi, 1990; Hirschi, 1969; Loeber and LaBlanc, 1990). Detachment is linked to problems in adolescence and adulthood such as, but not limited to, aggression, anger, risk-taking, decreased risk perceptions, impulsivity, delinquency, criminality, and other negative behaviors and life outcomes (Blackwell, 2000; Gottfredson and Hirschi, 1990; Hirschi, 1969; Loeber and Stouthamer-Loeber, 1986).

Hayslett-McCall and Bernard (2002), drawing from Gottfredson and Hirschi (1990), ultimately link early attachment to the development of self-control, concurring that strong attachments lead to higher levels of self-control and disrupted attachments produce low self-control. Specifically, Hayslett-McCall and Bernard note the similarities in discussions of parenting and its link to attachment across both developmental psychologists and Gottfredson and Hirschi. The notion that parents' lack of supervision, identification of behavioral problems, and/or appropriate response to behavioral problems relates to attachment and further psychological and behavioral problems is embraced in all these frameworks. Differences exist with regard to the ordering of the concepts. In the eyes of Gottfredson and Hirschi (1990), the affective attachment of the parents to their children (how much they care for them) determines the level of instrumental control the offspring obtains. The supervision and punishment practice then shapes the development of self-control. According to Hayslett-McCall and Bernard (2002), culturally rooted child-rearing practices affect (early) attachment to parents, which has an influence on the development of (low) self-control, which ultimately generates criminal behavior.

The key component of Hayslett-McCall and Bernard's (2002) gendered attachment–self-control theory is the linkages they identify between gendered socialization patterns and the production of self-control. Drawing from masculinities and feminist research (Chodorow, 1978, 1989; Messerschmidt, 1993; Pleck, 1995), they assert that parents interact differently with boys and girls, yielding systematically different levels of attachment across the sexes. More specifically, it is argued that boys in today's society are expected to separate from their mothers, but because their fathers are both physically and emotionally removed, no replacement attachments occur. Moreover, Hayslett-McCall and Bernard (2002: 16-17) note that the expectations of independence and risk-taking, which are associated with masculinity, are further "taught" to boys through a socialization process that "discourage(s) and reject(s) expressions of vulnerability and dependency from boys at a very early age…," thus emphasizing "a cultural image of manliness or masculinity that does not include (these) relational elements …." Meanwhile, parental socialization of girls maintains an emphasis on the importance of forming attachments and relationships, expectations that are associated with the feminine gender role. All this leads to girls having stronger early attachments to caregivers than boys.

In brief: the main argument of Hayslett-McCall and Bernard's (2002) approach to explaining the gender gap in juvenile delinquency is that, on the grounds of culturally underpinned gendered child-rearing practices, boys experience more disruptions in early attachments to primary care-givers, which leads to them developing less self-control and consequently a higher propensity to offend.

In their wording, Hayslett-McCall and Bernard focus heavily on early secure attachment to primary caregivers, but this argument can be extended to encompass maternal or parental attachment in general. By maintaining that "attachments can be re-established in later life" (2002: 7), they themselves hint to such a broader understanding.

Finally, it is important to note that while Hayslett-McCall and Bernard (2002) link socialization into gender roles with the (non-)formation of appropriate attachments to parents, they also recognize that not all boys are subjected to "traumatic" detachment processes. Rather, they contend that as mothers begin detachment processes with boys, if boys are able to form new attachments with involved fathers or other, particularly male, figures, traumatic detachment may be avoided. With this, they account for the influence of aggregate level factors, such as family composition, neighborhood disorganization, and even the effects of mass incarceration.

Unfortunately, to date, while over 20 studies have cited Hayslett-McCall and Bernard's theory, none provides an actual assessment of the model (see e.g. Alexander et al., 2004; Costello and Mederer, 2003). Instead, most references to Hayslett-McCall and Bernard's theory focus on their discussion of the role of attachment in either anti-social outcomes generally, or the variance of such outcomes across the sexes. Explicit tests of their models are not offered. However, tests of Gottfredson and Hirschi's general theory that explore the gender-self-control-crime relationship provide relevant findings in this regard.

Gender, Parenting, and Low Self-Control

Recall that Gottfredson and Hirschi (1990) posited that females would have higher levels of self-control than their male counterparts, largely as a result of their different socialization experiences. Boys were expected to develop lower self-control than females due to gender differences in parenting. Specifically, it was anticipated that boys would be more likely to be subjected to ineffective parenting techniques – lack of monitoring, recognition of deviance, and corrective action – than girls.

Research has generated typically supportive results for these claims. Self-control differences between the sexes have been widely established. Several studies demonstrate that girls, compared to boys, have higher levels of self-control (Burton et al., 1998; LaGrange and Silverman, 1999; Marshall and Enzmann, 2012). It has also been shown that self-control can partially explain the gender gap in criminal behavior. The gender ratio in offending seems to result from the gender difference in self-control, at least so some extent (Burton et al., 1998; LaGrange and Silverman, 1999; Tittle et al., 2003).

There is also ample evidence that girls receive more instrumental and relational control from their parents than boys. Parents are more likely to make daughters the target of their supervision and to form close emotional bonds to them. Sons are less likely than daughters to be the object of parental monitoring and affection (Armsden and Greenberg, 1987; Blackwell and Reed, 2003; Hadjar et al., 2007; Hagan et al., 1985; 1987; Hirtenlehner et al., 2014a).

Research on the etiology of low self-control confirms that ineffective parenting as described by Gottfredson and Hirschi is a major cause of low self-control (Cullen et al., 2008; Gottfredson 2006). However, findings also indicate that the relationship between parenting and the development of self-control is more complex than initially assumed.

For example, while Gibbs et al. (1998) report that parenting strategies did not vary across boys and girls, other studies have reported gendered variations in parenting practices. In an early gendered test of self-control theory, Blackwell and Piquero (2005) reported that supervision/monitoring was an important predictor of self-control across both sexes; both men and women reported higher levels of self-control associated with higher levels of parental monitoring. However, they further observed that a measure of attachment, or affection, had variant effects on the development of self-control, depending on the genders of the parent-child attachment dyad. In particular, girls who had high levels of paternal affection had higher levels of self-control than girls attached to their mothers and boys regardless of parent. In contrast, Chapple et al. (2010) found that while maternal controls were important for increasing self control for both boys and girls, maternal attachment/affection was more predictive of boy's self-control than that of girls. Thus, while findings seem to support Gottfredson and Hirschi's position that appropriate monitoring and supervision is necessary for children's development of self-control, attachment to parent's also plays a role (Nofziger, 2008; Pratt et al., 2004; Turner et al., 2005). Several studies demonstrate correlations between parental attachment and self-control, with children or adolescents receiving more parental affection reporting higher levels of self-control (Flexon et al., 2012; Hope et al., 2003; Marshall and Enzmann, 2012; Ventura Miller et al., 2009; Wright and Beaver, 2005).

Gottfredson and Hirschi's model posits that the effect of parental control on delinquency and crime is indirect, through self-control. While research sometimes supports this claim (Blackwell and Piquero, 2005; Chapple et al., 2010; Keane et al., 1993; Vazsonyi and Bellison, 2007), some studies have pointed out that parental controls also have a direct effect on crime and delinquency (Chapple et al., 2010; Hay, 2001; Marshall and Enzmann, 2012; Unnever et al., 2003).

Ample evidence suggests that low self-control is a powerful predictor of offending – although not the only one, as proposed by Gottfredson and Hirschi (1990). Individuals who lack self-control are more likely to engage in criminal and analogous behaviors than people with high self-control (Evans et al., 1997; Grasmick et al., 1993; Marshall and Enzmann, 2012; Pratt and Cullen, 2000; Rebellon et al., 2008; Vazsonyi et al., 2001).

The linkages between parental attachment, self-control and juvenile delinquency, as they are outlined by Hayslett-McCall and Bernard (2002), have been established in a cross-sectional study from Puerto Rico (Ventura Miller et al., 2009).

This work shows that low self-control partially mediates the effect of weak maternal attachment on adolescents' deviant behavior, but is based on a self-control theory framework and does not even cite Hayslett-McCall and Bernard' account.

In sum, a review of the literature on self-control indicates a need for a broader and deeper understanding not only of gender differences in crime and delinquency, but also of Gottfredson and Hirschi's position that self-control varies across boys and girls solely because of gendered differences in parental monitoring. Indeed, consistent with Hayslett-McCall and Bernard's argument, research indicates that parental attachment varies across both the parents who give affection and the children who receive it. These differences in affection appear to work in a significantly more complex manner to generate variability in self-control than originally posited by Gottfredson and Hirschi (1990). Hayslett-McCall and Bernard, through their gendered attachment–self-control theory, offer a theoretical framework to enhance our understanding of the complexities of these relationships. This study presents an initial examination of this explanation.

METHOD

Data

Our attempt to test key propositions of the gendered attachment–self-control theory utilizes data from a school-administered online survey of 2,911 students in the 7th and 8th grades. This survey was conducted in two Austrian provinces in 2011. As expected given the grades in which surveys were administered, respondents predominately were between 13 and 14 years old.

Data collection was based on a multi-stage sampling plan. At stage 1, a disproportionally stratified random sample of 50 schools from Upper Austria and 42 schools from Lower Austria was selected[2]. School type was employed

---

[2] To realize a net sample of 92 schools, 115 schools had to be contacted. This corresponds to a participation rate of 80.

as stratification variable[3]. At stage 2, a random selection of one 7th and one 8th grade class per school was taken.

Table 1. Sample composition (n = 2,911)

Characteristic	Unweighted data	Weighted data
Sex		
Boys	52%	50%
Girls	48%	50%
Age		
12 years	19%	21%
13 years	43%	43%
14 years	32%	30%
15 or more years	6%	6%
Grade		
7th class	50%	50%
8th class	50%	50%
Province		
Upper Austria	58%	49%
Lower Austria	42%	51%

At stage 3, all students attending the selected classes were targeted. Absences and refusals to take part in the survey yielded a final coverage rate of 86%. The composition of the final sample is reported in Table 1.

The online survey was conducted during class hours in the schools' computer rooms[4]. Each class was led to the computer room to complete the survey under the instruction of trained interviewers. Teachers were present during the investigation to maintain discipline. Interviewers ensured that the teachers could not see students' responses.

Measurement

Delinquency: Self-reported offending, the key response variable, was measured utilizing a variety scale. The scale depicts the number of different

[3] In Austria, for the age groups surveyed here, three types of schools are available: grammar schools, comprehensive schools and schools for children with special needs. Due to their small number, grammar schools and schools for children with special needs were oversampled.

[4] The questionnaire was implemented with the online research tool EFS Survey (www.unipark.com).

offenses a respondent has committed in the year before the survey[5]. The nine included crimes were:

- spraying graffiti on another person‘s or public property,
- wilfully damaging or destroying things not belonging to the respondent,
- stealing anything from a shop,
- stealing anything from another person,
- selling or buying stolen things,
- threatening or extorting someone to take money or other things from him,
- hitting or beating up someone,
- violently taking money or other things from another person,
- breaking into someone‘s house or flat to steal something.

In total, 37% of the respondents reported engagement in at least one of the studied crimes in the past 12 months.

Self-control: The extent of self-control was measured by a modified and abridged version of the self-control scale developed by Grasmick and colleagues (1993). The six items tap particularly, but not exclusively, into the impulsivity and risk-taking components of the construct, which has been empirically demonstrated to be closely correlated with offending (Arneklev et al., 1993; Longshore et al., 1996; Vazsonyi et al., 2001)[6]. Responses provided on a four-point Likert scale ["strongly disagree" (0) – "strongly agree" (3)] were summed and coded so that high scores on the summated scale indicate high self-control (Cronbach's alpha = .63).

Maternal Attachment: To measure attachment to the primary caregiver, we drew on the adolescent's relationship to the mother. Respondents were asked how close they feel to their mother [with responses coded between "not close at all" (0) and "very close" (3)] and how often they talk to her about their thoughts and feelings [with responses coded between "never" (0) and "always"

---

[5] We rely on a measure of the versatility of offending, since it has been shown that variety scales outperform frequency scales in many respects (Bendixen et al., 2003).

[6] The following items were utilized to create this composite scale: "I often act on the spur of the moment without stopping to think"; "I often try to avoid things that I know will be difficult"; "I lose my temper pretty easily"; "When I am really angry, other people better stay away from me"; "I often take a risk just for the fun of it"; "Sometimes I find it exciting to do things that are dangerous."

(3)]. Items were summed to create the composite *Maternal Attachment* measure (r = .44; p = .000).

Admittedly, this operationalization captures bonding to the mother at age 13 or 14, which may be different from attachment to the primary caregiver in early years. However, this is justified given the stability of the attachment style formed in early childhood. According to Bowlby (1969; 1988), the type of attachment established between mother and child in the first year of life translates into a general attachment style that shapes an individual's bonding behaviors in adolescence and adulthood. Continuity may be assumed for both the descendant's and mother's bonding behaviors; when spared from mental diseases or serious deteriorations of outer living conditions, an initially affectionate and caring mother will also meet her older children with love and devotion. From this perspective, later attachment to the mother may well serve as a proxy measure of early attachment to her.

Male: Sex was coded 0 for girls and 1 for boys.

Besides the concepts central to the examined theory, several control variables were incorporated into the study.

Paternal Attachment: To make sure that attachment to the mother does not act as a proxy for attachment to the father, the latter was included in the analysis. *Paternal attachment* was generated utilizing indicators parallel to those employed for maternal attachment. "Feeling close to the father" and "talking to the father about one's thoughts and feelings" proved to be clearly associated (r = .43; p = .000). To construct a composite measure, both items were summed.

Morality: Moral beliefs, i.e. adolescents' personal attitudes towards rule-breaking, were tapped through 10 statements utilized to assess respondents' perceptions of different forms of wrongdoing. The forms of rule-breaking ranged in seriousness from "riding a bike through a red light" or "skipping school without an excuse" to "breaking into a building to steal something" or "hitting another young person who makes a rude comment"[7]. For each type of misbehavior, respondents utilized a four-point Likert scale, ranging from "not at all wrong" (coded 0) to "very wrong" (coded 3), to indicate their perception of the behavior. The final scale is an additive index with an alpha of .82. It was coded so that high scores indicate elevated levels of morality.

[7] The other six forms of wrongdoing incorporated in the scale were "teasing a classmate because of the way he or she dresses," "getting drunk with friends on weekends," "stealing a pencil from a classmate," "painting graffiti on a house wall," "smashing a street light for fun" and "stealing a CD from a shop."

Deterrence: Perceptual deterrence was measured in terms of the perceived risk of apprehension. Since research indicates that the likelihood of being sanctioned is a better predictor of offending than sanctioning severity (Paternoster, 2010; Pratt et al., 2006), certainty of punishment was selected as the focus of this research. Respondents were asked to estimate the risk of being caught when (a) stealing a CD from a shop or (b) breaking into a car to steal something ($r = .44$; $p = .000$). A four-point Likert scale, ranging from "no risk at all" (coded 0) to "a very great risk" (coded 3), was used to record responses. An index was created by summating item scores; high values denote more deterrence[8].

Table 2 provides the correlations between all variables included in the analysis.

Analysis

Complex samples are characterized by a multi-stage sampling design with clusterings and stratifications on several stages of selection. Since the present data rests on such a complex sampling plan, all analyses were performed considering this complex sample mode. We employed the Taylor series method (Lee and Forthofer, 2006) to obtain unbiased standard errors and significance levels.

All analyses were conducted with a weighted data set. First, design weights were calculated to correct for distortions resulting from the sampling plan. Then the design weights were expanded with post-stratification weights to ensure representativeness.

Post-stratification was based jointly on province, grade and gender. As demonstrated in Table 1, changes in the structure of the data only occurred with regard to regional composition. The fact that, against the backdrop of nearly equivalent numbers of students in both provinces, the school authority of Lower Austria was more restrictive in allowing schools to take part in the survey than its Upper Austrian counterpart was corrected by the post-stratification adjustment.

[8] The problem that deterrence perceptions were observed for property crimes only is partially defused by the fact that other studies utilizing a more heterogeneous set of crimes to determine overall detection risk attest these more crime-diverse scales a high level of internal consistency (Hirtenlehner et al., 2014b; Pauwels et al., 2011; Svensson, 2015). For scales combining property and violent crimes to assess perceived detection risk, Cronbach's alpha usually exceeds .70.

Table 2. Product-moment correlations

Variable	1.	2.	3.	4.	5.	6.	7.
1.Crime variety	1.00	----	----	----	----	----	----
2. Self-control	-.41***	1.00	----	----	----	----	----
3. Attachment to mother	-.24***	+.27***	1.00	----	----	----	----
4. Sex	+.19***	-.12***	-.18***	1.00	----	----	----
5. Morality	-.48***	+.41**	+.36***	-.10***	1.00	----	----
6. Perceived deterrence	-.43***	+.32***	+.22***	-.24***	+.46***	1.00	----
7. Attachment to father	-.15***	+.17***	+.48***	+.08**	+.25***	+.10***	1.00

* $p \leq .05$; ** $p \leq .01$; *** $p \leq .001$.

Model estimation was conducted using Mplus 6 (Muthén and Muthén, 2010), which enables fitting path models with differently scaled variables. Since the final outcome variable, crime variety, represents a count variable marked by serious overdispersion[9], a negative binomial regression had to be integrated in the path model. The latter renders the calculation of standardized regression coefficients for the full model impossible.

Hence, only unstandardized regression coefficients are reported. Apart from crime variety, all variables were z-standardized before entering them into the equations to allow the regression coefficients between all variables, other than "versatility of crime," to be interpreted as standardized coefficients. The regression weights on the crime scale are at least comparable[10].

RESULTS

The analysis begins with an investigation of the gendered nature of the concepts employed in Hayslett-McCall and Bernard's account of the male crime surplus. Table 3 presents findings on the gendered distribution of offending, self-control and attachment to the mother. All bivariate differences conform to the theoretical expectations. Specifically, boys are more likely to

[9] According to a Lagrange multiplier test, fitting a Poisson regression is thwarted by a significant overdispersion of the crime variety measure ($p \leq .001$).

[10] Fitting all the equations simultaneously was possible only by implementing Monte-Carlo integration (Muthén and Muthén, 2010: 418 ff.).

engage in criminal behavior than girls. Approximately half of the boys report having committed at least one of the requested crimes in the last 12 months. The same applies only to a quarter of the girls participating in the survey. The average score on the versatility scale is twice as high for boys as it is for girls. Concerning the emphasized predictor variables, it is apparent that boys report both lower levels of self-control and less attachment to the mother than girls. All differences prove to be highly significant.

Table 3. Gendered distribution of theoretical concepts

Variable	Boys	Girls	Δ	p
1-year-prevalence of delinquency	48%	26%	22%	.000
Crime variety (∅)	0.97	0.48	+0.49	.000
Self-control (∅)	9.21	10.01	-0.80	.000
Attachment to mother (∅)	3.22	3.73	-0.51	.000

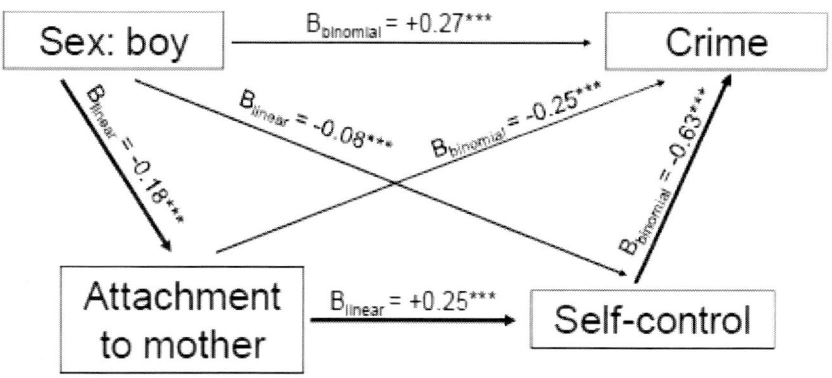

B_{linear} = regression coefficient from linear model.
$B_{binomial}$ = regression coefficient from negative binomial model.
$^{***}p \leq .001$, $^{**}p \leq .01$, $^{*}p \leq .05$.

Figure 1. Empirical path model.

In a next step, attention is shifted to the inter-relationships between the theoretical concepts. To determine whether the covariance structures inherent in the data are consistent with several predictions derived from a gendered attachment–self-control theory, a path model was estimated. The specified model assumes that gender affects bonding with the mother, which in turn varies with level of self-control, the latter impacting directly on criminal involvement. Additional pathways between the constructs are explicitly allowed. Figure 1 gives the results.

It is apparent from the path diagram that the empirical covariances between the concepts are very much in line with the gendered attachment–self-control theory. Gender relates to maternal attachment, with boys experiencing more disruptions than their female counterparts. Reduced attachment to the mother likewise is associated with reduced self-control. Finally, low self-control, in turn, fosters offending.

The gender–attachment–self-control–crime chain is crucial to the understanding of the gendered distribution of juvenile delinquency. Effect sizes beyond this chain are much smaller than the ones producing the described linkage.

Nevertheless, the findings also indicate that sex and maternal attachment have independent effects on crime variety, with being male and a lack of bonding increasing delinquent behavior. The fact that gender retains a direct association with offending after the theoretically postulated mediating factors are controlled implies that Hayslett-McCall and Bernard's approach does not fully account for the gender gap in criminal involvement[11].

The inadequacy of the base model in explaining the gender divide in criminal conduct suggests including more independent variables. Drawing from prior research, moral beliefs, perceived deterrence and attachment to the father were introduced as additional predictors.

In Western societies, usually the mother acts as primary caregiver for the offspring, but the father's significance in childrearing is increasing, especially as children grow older (Hagan 1989; Blackwell, 2000; Grasmick, et al., 1996). To separate the effects of disruptions in early attachment to primary caregivers

---

[11] At this juncture, a few technical remarks are warranted. At first it must be noted that, since all predictor variables in the model are z-standardized, effect sizes can be compared with each other. The fact that the effects of these predictors on crime variety are estimated in terms of a negative binomial regression, though, renders it impossible to determine how much the initial impact of gender on delinquency is reduced by adjusting the analysis for maternal attachment and self-control. This is why we re-estimated the path model in purely linear terms. Substantively identical results are obtained with this model. Specifying the last equation in a linear framework yields an unstandardized gender regression coefficient of .49 in a sex-only model, which drops to .31 in the full model. From this it follows that introducing maternal attachment and self-control in the model reduces the gender–crime relationship by 37%, or, in brief, that the mediating variables emphasized by the theory can explain more than a third of the initial gender gradient of juvenile delinquency. Regarding goodness-of-fit it must be clarified that Mplus does not provide efficient fit criteria for path models with differently scaled variables. An ordinary least squares regression on crime variety indicates that the three predictors together can explain 20% of the variation in juvenile offending.

from the impact of paternal bonding efforts, measures of both concepts must simultaneously be included in explanatory models.

Table 4 presents the results from regressing crime variety on the full range of predictors available for the analysis, again in a negative binomial framework. These findings replicate and reinforce the previous conclusions. Strong moral beliefs and high perceived risks of detection decrease offending, but low self-control remains the most powerful predictor.

On the other hand, Gottfredson and Hirschi's (1990) assumption that correlations between delinquency and other factors are spurious, reflecting only their joint dependency on the ability to exercise self-control, is refuted by the data. Both maternal and paternal attachment exhibit weak, but significant, direct associations with offending. The effect sizes of these measures are nearly identical in magnitude, and are considerably lower than those of the other predictors. Results of the linear model regressing self-control on attachment to parents and gender are reported in Table 5.

Table 4. Determinants of crime frequency (negative binomial models)

	B	Z
Sex	+0.22***	5.78
Self-control	-0.39***	10.98
Attachment to mother	-0.09*	2.09
Morality	-0.36***	9.07
Perceived deterrence	-0.27***	7.60
Attachment to father	-0.09*	2.13

*p ≤ .05; **p ≤ .01; ***p ≤ .001. B - unstandardized regression coefficient; Z - Z-statistic
All predictor variables are z-standardized.

Table 5. Determinants of self-control (linear regression model)

	Beta	Z
Sex: boy	-.09***	4.04
Attachment to mother	+.23***	9.18
Attachment to father	+.07**	2.72
Determination coefficient R^2	.09***	

*p ≤ .05; **p ≤ .01; ***p ≤ .001.
Beta - standardized regression coefficient; Z - Z-statistic.

These results indicate that maternal attachment, here serving as a proxy for attachment to the primary caregiver in early childhood, is the best predictor of an individual's level of self-control. Attachment to the father plays a minor role; it is significantly, but not substantially, linked to the ability to exercise self-control.

The fact that bonding to the mother clearly 'trumps' bonding to the father in its association with self-control backs both the assumed causal ordering of the constructs and the employed measurement strategy[13].

Taken together, the regression models displayed in Tables 4 and 5 suggest that the impact chain postulated by the gendered attachment–self-control theory holds when the analysis is adjusted for additional influencing factors. The expanded model, however, still does not fully account for gender differences in the likelihood of offending. Sex retains a significant direct effect on delinquency, which indicates that concepts not included in our analyses also contribute to the formation of the corresponding gender gap.

Finally, 'gender ratio' problem studies on the gendered nature of criminal behavior also call for researchers to address the generalizability issue, i.e. the capacity of a theory to explain offending equally well for males and females (Iovanni and Miller 2008). Along these lines, both self-control and crime frequency were regressed on the familiar predictors separately for boys and girls (Table 6). The results show that the inner workings of the attachment–self-control model are roughly the same for both sexes.

Strong attachment to the mother goes together with an elevated level of self-control for both boys and girls, whereas the effects of bonding to the father are either insignificant or negligible. This is consistent with the notion that attachment to the primary caregiver in early childhood shapes the development of self-control among sons and daughters. Against the backdrop of the previous observation that boys report less attachment to the mother and less self-control than girls, these findings thus corroborate a key proposition of the tested theory.

Self-control, in turn, emerges as an influential, but not lone, predictor of criminal behavior. Among boys, self-control is approximately as predictive as personal morality and perceived deterrence; among girls, only moral beliefs match self-control in explanatory power. In combination with the afore-

[13] There is no plausible reason for the assumption that level of self-control exerts a much greater influence on attachment to the mother than it does on attachment to the father. The difference in the effect sizes is, however, very compatible with the supposition that early attachment to primary caregivers matters more for personality development than later bonding to the father.

mentioned fact that boys report both less self-control and more crime than girls, these effect dynamics substantiate another core argument of the examined theory.

Table 6. Determinants of self-control and crime frequency differentiated by sex

	Dependent variable: Self-control (linear model)				Dependent variable: Crime variety (negative binomial model)			
	Boys		Girls		Boys		Girls	
Variable	Beta	Z	Beta	Z	B	Z	B	Z
Attachment to mother	+.20***	5.50	+.24***	6.60	-0.07	1.32	-0.11	1.50
Attachment to father	+.06	1.66	+.09*	2.19	-0.03	0.61	-0.21**	3.09
Self-control					-0.34***	8.14	-0.43***	6.19
Morality					-0.30***	6.08	-0.46***	7.51
Perceived deterrence					-0.31***	7.24	-0.21***	3.50

*$p \leq .05$; **$p \leq .01$; ***$p \leq .001$.

B - unstandardized regression coefficient; Beta - standardized regression coefficient; Z - Z-statistic All predictor variables are z-standardized.

Discussion

This article tested core propositions of Hayslett-McCall and Bernard's gendered attachment–self-control theory (2002), an empirically neglected approach to explaining the gender gap in criminal behavior.

On balance, the results of a student crime survey from Austria support the specified explanatory model. Compared to girls, boys report more offending and lower levels of both self-control and attachment to the mother. The correlational structures between these concepts correspond to the theoretical expectations, with disruptions in attachment to the mother facilitating a lack of self-control, and weak self-control fostering criminal conduct. These relationships remain stable when additional covariates are taken into account, but do not fully account for the gender gradient of juvenile delinquency.

Concerning the assumption of culturally underpinned gendered parenting techniques in early childhood, no inferences can be made from this study. The scant German-speaking literature on the role of gender in attachment theory, though, suggests that, regarding the mother, attachment quality is the same for boys and girls in their first two years of life (Grossmann 1989; Spangler and Grossmann 1993). It is not before an age of about two years that gendered pathways of maternal sensitivity and behavior begin to unfold (Kindler 2011). These pathways may well result in young boys being more exposed to attachment-debilitating childrearing techniques than young girls. There is, for example, evidence that, in adolescence, Austrian girls receive more relational and instrumental control from their mother than their male counterparts (Hirtenlehner et al. 2014a). Additionally, it is presumed that the chances to compensate early attachment deficits, e.g. with the help of other attachment figures, vary by gender – with girls less likely to suffer long-term negative consequences than boys (Kunstmann 2010).

This study does offer important implications reinforcing Hayslett-McCall and Bernard's position that parental attachment is much more complex than previously thought, in both its development and its impact on a variety of mechanisms that may push youth into offending or hold youth back. Indeed, the relative lack of depth in criminological research exploring attachment to others became clear in reviewing these literatures. Despite recognition of the importance of parents across theoretical paradigms, including not only control theories but also strain and learning theories, it is somewhat surprising that the constructs and measures of attachment remain so rudimentary in nature, preventing a deeper understanding of the role of parental attachment in generating traits and proclivities that impact future delinquency and crime. Future research on this issue will be well-advised to develop a more elaborate conceptualization of attachment to significant others and work out better measures that fully capture the concept.

The gender-crime literature provides an ideal avenue to pursue an enhanced understanding of the role played by our attachment to others, not the least as this literature submitted evidence that attachments to fathers and mothers may have differential impacts on girls and boys. These findings, added to the theoretical underpinnings outlined by Hayslett-McCall and Bernard (2002), suggest that, particularly within control theory frameworks, there is a need to more deeply examine boys' attachments to fathers and mothers in comparison to those of girls'. Indeed, research on power-control theory (Blackwell, 2000; Blackwell and Piqureo, 2005) has suggested that rather than focusing on the role of mothers and their impacts on girls attachments to understand the gender-crime gap, the focus should be on the father-son attachment bond, as it is the strength of these attachments that reduce the gender-crime gap.

The present study is subject to several methodological limitations. To begin, the cross-sectional nature of the research is salient. Assessment of a dynamic developmental theory targeted at explaining the formation of the propensity to offend on the basis of 'snapshot' data from a single point in time is perhaps an overly ambitious endeavor. In our defense, as far as we know, this investigation is the first one explicitly dedicated to examining Hayslett-McCall and Bernard's perspective on the gendered distribution of criminal conduct.

Cross-sectional studies can mark a good starting point to empirically tackle a theory, gain first insights into its compatibility with social reality, and stimulate subsequent longitudinal research.

Further, it is worth noting that, due to our cross-sectional design, with current level of bonding to the mother only a proxy measure of early attachment to the primary caregiver is available. With the stability of the attachment style on both the mother's and the descendant's side, attachment theory (Bowlby 1988) itself provides a rationale for our employment of this operationalization strategy. Nevertheless, future research on the gendered attachment–self-control theory is advised to draw on a longitudinal design.

Criticism regarding the temporal ordering of self-control and offending (the former is measured at the moment of the survey, the latter for the year preceding the survey) can be countered by referring to the theoretical conceptualization of self-control as an enduring personality trait in Hayslett-McCall and Bernard's account[14].

REFERENCES

Ainsworth, M. (1972). Attachment and Dependency. In: J. Gewirtz (Ed.), *Attachment and Dependency* (pp. 97–137). Washington: Winston.

Alexander, F., Allen, C., Brooks, J., Cole, C., and Campbell, A. (2004). Reason to Believe: Representations of Aggression as Phenomenological Read-Out. *Sex Roles*, 11/12, 647-659.

Armsden, G. and Greenberg, M. (1987). The Inventory of Parent and Peer Attachment: Individual Differences and Their Relationship to

[14] The same applies, of course, to Gottfredson and Hirschi's General Theory of Crime (1990).

Psychological Well-Being in Adolescence. *Journal of Youth and Adolescence* 16, 427–454.

Arneklev, B., Grasmick, H., Tittle, C., and Bursik, R. (1993). Low Self-Control and Imprudent Behavior. *Journal of Quantitative Criminology* 9, 225–239.

Bendixen, M., Endresen, I. and Olweus, D. (2003). Variety and Frequency Scales of Antisocial Involvement: Which One is better? *Legal and Criminological Psychology* 8, 135–150.

Blackwell, B. S. (2000). Perceived Sanction Threats, Gender, and Crime: A Test and Elaboration of Power-Control Theory. *Criminology* 38, 439–488.

Blackwell, B. S. and Piquero, A. (2005). On the Relationships Between Gender, Power Control, Self-Control, and Crime. *Journal of Criminal Justice* 33, 1–17.

Blackwell, B. S. and Reed, M. (2003). Power-Control as a Between- and Within-Family Model: Reconsidering the Unit of Analysis. *Journal of Youth and Adolescence* 32, 385–400.

Bowlby, J. (1969). *Attachment and Loss. Volume 1: Attachment.* New York: Harper.

Bowlby, J. (1988). *A Secure Base: Parent-Child Attachment and Healthy Human Development.* New York: Basic Books.

Burton, V., et al. (1998). Gender, Self-Control, and Crime. *Journal of Research in Crime and Delinquency* 25, 123–147.

Chapple, C., Vaske, J. and Hope, T. (2010). Sex Differences in the Causes of Self-Control: An Examination of Mediation, Moderation, and Gender Etiologies. *Journal of Criminal Justice* 38, 1122–1131.

Chodorow, N. (1978). *The Reproduction of Mothering: Psychoanalysis and the Sociology of Gender.* Berkeley, CA: University of California Press.

Chodorow, N. (1989). *Feminism and Psychoanalytic Theory.* New Haven: Yale University Press.

Costello, B. and Mederer, H. (2003). A Control Theory of Gender Difference in Crime and Delinquency. In: C. Britt and M. Gottfredson (Eds.), *Control Theories of Crime and Delinquency* (pp. 77–107). New Brunswick: Transaction.

Evans, T., Cullen, F., Burton, V., Dunaway, R., and Benson, M. (1997). The Social Consequences of Self-Control: Testing the General Theory of Crime. *Criminology* 35, 475–504.

Flexon, J., Greenleaf, R. and Lurigio, A. (2012). The Effects of Self-Control, Gang-Membership, and Parental Attachment/Identification on Police

Contacts Among Latino and African American Youths. *International Journal of Offender Therapy and Comparative Criminology* 56, 218–238.

Gibbs, J., Giever, D. and Martin, J. (1998). Parental Management and Self-Control: An Empirical Test of Gottfredson and Hirschi's General Theory. *Journal of Research in Crime and Delinquency* 35, 40–70.

Gilligan, C. (1982). *In a Different Voice.* Harvard University Press.

Gottfredson, M. (2006). The Empirical Status of Control Theory in Criminology. In: F. Cullen, J. Wright and K. Blevins (Eds.), *Taking Stock. The Status of Criminological Theory* (pp. 77–100). New Brunswick: Transaction.

Gottfredson, M. and Hirschi, T. (1990). *A General Theory of Crime.* Stanford: Stanford University Press.

Grasmick, H., Hagan, J., Blackwell, B., and Arneklev, B. (1996). Risk Preferences and Patriarchy: Extending power-control theory. *Social Forces* 75, 177–199.

Grasmick, H., Tittle, C., Bursick, R., and Arneklev, B. (1993). Testing the Core Empirical Implications of Gottfredson and Hirschi's General Theory of Crime. *Journal of Research in Crime and Delinquency* 30, 5–29.

Grossmann, K. (1989). *Differential Effects of Attachment Quality to Mother and Father on Boys and Girls.* Paper presented on the 10th Biennial Meeting of the International Society for the Study of Behavioral Development.

Hadjar, A., Baier, D., Boehnke, K., and Hagan, J. (2007). Juvenile Delinquency and Gender Revisited. The Family and Power-Control Theory Reconceived. *European Journal of Criminology* 4, 33–58.

Hagan, J. (1989). *Structural Criminology.* New Brunswick: Rutgers University Press.

Hagan, J., Gillis, A. R. and Simpson, J. (1985). The Class Structure of Gender and Delinquency: Toward a Power-Control Theory of Common Delinquent Behavior. *American Journal of Sociology* 90, 1151–1178.

Hagan, J., Simpson, J. and Gillis, A. R. (1987). Class in the Household: A Power-Control Theory of Gender and Delinquency. *American Journal of Sociology* 92, 788–816.

Hay, C. and Forest, W. (2006). The Development of Self-Control: Examining Self-Control Theory's Stability Thesis. *Criminology* 44, 739–774.

Hayslett-McCall, K. and Bernard, T. (2002). Attachment, Masculinity, and Self-control: A Theory of Male Crime Rates. *Theoretical Criminology* 6, 5–33.

Heimer, K. (1996). Gender, Interaction, and Delinquency: Testing a Theory of Differential Social Control. *Social Psychology Quarterly* 59, 39–61.

Heimer, K. and Matsueda, R. (1994). Role-taking, Role Commitment, and Delinquency: A Theory of Differential Social Control. *American Sociological Review* 59 365–390.

Hirschi, T. (1969). Causes of Delinquency. Berkeley: University of California Press.

Hirtenlehner, H., Blackwell, B., Leitgoeb, H., and Bacher, J. (2014a). Explaining the Gender Gap in Juvenile Shoplifting: A Power-Control Theoretical Analysis. *Deviant Behavior* 35, 41–65.

Hirtenlehner, H., Pauwels, R. and Mesko, G. (2014b). Is the Effect of Perceived Deterrence on Juvenile Offending Contingent on the Level of Self-Control? Results from Three Countries. *British Journal of Criminology* 54, 128–150.

Hope, T., Grasmick, H. and Pointon, L. (2003). The Family in Gottfredson and Hirschi's General Theory of Crime: Structure, Parenting, and Self-Control. *Sociological Focus* 36, 291–311.

Iovanni, L. and Miller, S. (2008). A Feminist Consideration of Gender and Crime. In: E. Goode (Ed.), *Out of Control. Assessing the General Theory of Crime* (pp. 127–141). Stanford: Stanford University Press.

Junger-Tas, J., Ribeaud, D. and Cruyff, M. (2004). Juvenile Delinquency and Gender. *European Journal of Criminology* 1, 333–375.

Keane, C., Maxim, P. and Teevan, J. (1993). Drinking and Driving, Self-Control, and Gender. *Journal of Research in Crime and Delinquency* 30, 30–46.

Kindler, H. (2011). Geschlechtsbezogene Aspekte der Bindungsentwicklung. In: G. Spangler and P. Zimmermann (Eds.), *Die Bindungstheorie. Grundlagen, Forschung und Anwendung* (pp. 281–296). Stuttgart, Germany: Klett-Cotta.

Kunstmann, A. C. (2010). *Familiale Verbundenheit und Gerechtigkeit.* Wiesbaden, Germany: VS Verlag für Sozialwissenschaften.

LaGrange, T. and Silverman, R. (1999). Low Self-Control and Opportunity: Testing the General Theory of Crime as an Explanation for Gender Differences in Delinquency. *Criminology* 37, 41–72.

Lee, E. and Forthofer, R. (2006). *Analyzing Complex Survey Data*. London: Sage.

Loeber, R. and LaBlanc, M. (1990). Toward a Developmental Criminology. In: M. Tonry and N. Morris (Eds.), *Crime and Justice: A Review of Research*. Vol. 11 (pp. 29–150). Chicago: University of Chicago Press.

Loeber, R. and Stouthamer-Loeber, M. (1986). Family Factors as Correlates and Predictors of Juvenile Conduct Problems and Delinquency. In: M. Tonry and N. Morris (Eds.), *Crime and Justice: A Review of Research*. Vol. 7 (pp. 29–149). Chicago: University of Chicago Press.

Longshore, D., Turner Rand, S. and Stein, J. (1996). Self-Control in a Criminal Sample: An Examination of Construct Validity. *Criminology* 34, 209–228.

Marshall, I. H. and Enzmann, D. (2012). The Generalizability of Self-Control Theory. In: J. Junger-Tas et al. (Eds.), *The Many Faces of Youth Crime. Contrasting Theoretical Perspectives on Juvenile Delinquency Across Countries and Cultures* (pp. 285–325). New York: Springer.

Messerschmidt, J. (1993). *Masculinities and Crime. Critique and Reconceptualization of Theory*. Lanham: Rowman and Littlefield.

Moffitt, T., Caspi, A., Rutter, M., and Silva, P. (2001). *Sex Differences in Antisocial Behavior. Conduct Disorder, Delinquency, and Violence in the Dunedin Longitudinal Study*. Cambridge: Cambridge University Press.

Muthén, L. and Muthén, B. (2010). *Mplus User's Guide*. Sixth Edition. Los Angeles: Muthén and Muthén.

Nofziger, S. (2008). The "Cause" of Low Self-Control: The Influence of Maternal Self-Control. *Journal of Research in Crime and Delinquency* 45, 191–224.

Paternoster, R. (2010). How Much Do We Really Know About Criminal Deterrence? *Journal of Criminal Law and Criminology* 100, 765–824.

Pauwels, L., Weerman, F., Bruinsma, G., and Bernasco, W. (2011). Perceived Sanction Risk, Individual Propensity and Adolescent Offending: Assessing Key Findings from the Deterrence Literature in a Dutch Sample. *European Journal of Criminology* 8, 386–400.

Pleck, J. (1995). The Gender Role Strain Paradigm: An Update. In: R. Levant and W. Pollack (Eds.), *A New Psychology of Men* (pp. 11–32). New York: Basic Books.

Pratt, T., Turner, M. and Piquero, A. (2004). Parental Socialization and Community Context: A Longitudinal Analysis of the Structural Sources of Low Self-Control. *Journal of Research in Crime and Delinquency* 41, 219–243.

Pratt, T. and Cullen, F. (2000). The Empirical Status of Gottfredson and Hirschi's General Theory of Crime: A Meta-Analysis. *Criminology* 38, 931–964.

Pratt, T., Cullen, F., Blevins, K., Daigle, L., and Madensen, T. (2006). The Empirical Status of Deterrence Theory: A Meta-Analysis. In: F. Cullen, J.

Wright and K. Plevins (Eds.), *Taking Stock: The Status of Criminological Theory* (pp. 367–395). New Brunswick: Transaction.

Rebellon, C., Strauss, M. and Medeiros, R. (2008). Self-Control in Global Perspective: An Empirical Assessment of Gottfredson and Hirschi's General Theory Within and Across 32 National Settings. *European Journal of Criminology* 5, 331–362.

Spangler, G. and Grossmann, K. (1993). Biobehavioral Organization in Securely and Insecurely Attached Infants. *Child Development* 64, 1439–1450.

Steffensmeier, D. and Allan, E. (1996). Gender and Crime: Toward a Gendered Theory of Female Offending. *Annual Review of Sociology* 22, 459–487.

Svensson, R. (2015). An Examination of the Interaction Between Morality and Deterrence in Offending: A Research Note. *Crime and Delinquency* 61, 3–18.

Tittle, C., Ward, D. and Grasmick, H. (2003). Gender, Age, and Crime/ Deviance: A Challenge to Self-Control Theory. *Journal of Research in Crime and Delinquency* 40, 426–453.

Turner, M., Piquero, A. and Pratt, T. (2005). The School Context as a Source of Self-Control. *Journal of Criminal Justice* 33, 327–339.

Unnever, J., Cullen, F. and Pratt, T. (2003). Parental Management, ADHD, and Delinquency Involvement: Reassessing Gottfredson and Hirschi's General Theory. *Justice Quarterly* 20, 471–500.

Vazsonyi, A. and Bellison, L. (2007). The Family → Low Self-Control → Deviance: A Cross-Cultural and Cross-National Test of Self-Control Theory. *Criminal Justice and Behavior* 34, 505–530.

Vazsonyi, A., Pickering, E., Junger, M., and Hessing, T. (2001). An Empirical Test of a General Theory of Crime: A Four-Nation Comparative Study of Self-Control and the Prediction of Deviance. *Journal of Research in Crime and Delinquency* 38, 91–131.

Ventura Miller, H., Jennings, W., Alvarez-Rivera, L., and Lanza-Kaduce, L. (2009). Self-Control, Attachment, and Deviance Among Hispanic Adolescents. *Journal of Criminal Justice* 37, 77–84.

Wright, J. and Beaver, K. (2005). Do Parents Matter in Creating Self-Control in Their Children? A Genetically Informed Test of Low Self-Control. *Criminology* 43, 1169–1198.

INDEX

A

abuse, 48, 51
accessibility, 88
adaptation, 52
ADHD, 116
adjustment, 103
adolescents, 98, 99, 102
adulthood, 95, 102
adults, 47
African-American, 82, 85
age, vii, ix, 10, 11, 22, 23, 24, 27, 50, 51, 68, 73, 74, 77, 80, 81, 82, 83, 84, 85, 87, 89, 94, 95, 96, 100, 102, 110
agencies, ix, 61, 74, 75
aggression, 52, 95
aggressiveness, ix, 41, 42, 44
agriculture, 13, 15, 16, 17, 21, 64
alcohol abuse, 51
algorithm, viii, 2, 11, 46
alienation, 48
allele, 49, 51, 52, 65
altruism, 46, 57
anger, 47, 95
annual rate, 32, 35
antisocial behavior, 47, 50, 65
antisocial personality, 71
antisocial personality disorder, 71
arrest(s), ix, 65, 73, 76, 85
arteries, 6
assessment, 7, 78, 82, 86, 97
assets, 10, 18, 20
attachment, vii, x, 91, 92, 93, 94, 95, 96, 97, 98, 99, 101, 102, 104, 105, 106, 107, 108, 109, 110, 111
attachment theory, 92, 110, 111
attitudes, 56, 57, 102
Austria, x, 91, 92, 93, 99, 100, 103, 109
automatic stereotype activation, 87
autonomy, 49
awareness, 42, 87

B

base, 6, 7, 9, 10, 14, 34, 37, 38, 58, 61, 106
behavioral problems, 95
behaviors, 95, 98, 102
Belarus, 12
Belgorod, viii, 2, 11, 12, 13, 17, 18, 21, 22, 23, 25, 26, 28, 29, 30, 33, 36, 37
benefits, 14, 16, 17, 19, 44
bias, ix, 73, 74, 75, 76, 77, 78, 79, 80, 83, 84, 85, 86, 87, 88
biosocial factors, vii, ix, 41
birth rate, 10
births, 10
black women, 75, 85
blueprint, 60
bonding, 94, 102, 105, 106, 107, 108, 111
bonds, 95, 97

brain, 50, 52, 80
breakdown, 7, 9
buyer, 53

C

capitalism, 60, 89
caregivers, 96
Caucasus, viii, 2
causal relationship, 60
causality, ix, 42, 44, 47, 52, 53, 60, 61
causation, 94
Census, 10, 39
chemical, 13
Chicago, 114, 115
childhood, 102, 108, 109
childrearing, 106, 110
child-rearing practices, 92, 94, 95, 96
children, 45, 47, 93, 95, 98, 99, 100, 102, 106
cities, 5, 7
citizens, 6, 76, 77, 80, 82
classes, 100
classification, 7
classroom, 86
climate, 6
cluster analysis, 56
clusters, 56
cognitive activity, 75, 78, 79
cognitive bias, ix, 74, 76, 80
cognitive capacities, 60
cognitive function, 79
cognitive psychology, 43
common law, 7, 8
communication, 59, 60
community(s), 4, 59, 60
comparative method, viii, 2
compatibility, 111
compensation, 46
competition, 20, 44, 88
competitive advantage, 48, 49, 58, 63
complement, 53
complexity, 54, 59
composition, 96, 100, 103
comprehension, 3, 4
computer, 100
conceptualization, 110, 111
conditioning, 88
conductance, 43
configuration, 60, 61
conflict, 45
conformity, 50
consciousness, 78
construction, 49, 63
controversial, 75
cooperation, 47, 57, 65, 71
correlation(s), viii, 2, 3, 4, 42, 52, 57, 60, 78, 83, 87, 98, 103, 104, 107
cost, 89
crime-as-choice theory, ix, 41, 43, 44, 54, 57, 62
crime-facilitative culture, ix, 41, 44, 54, 60
crimes, vii, 1, 4, 27, 29, 31, 35, 61, 83, 101, 103, 105
criminal activity, ix, 74
criminal behavior, vii, x, 1, 47, 51, 65, 92, 95, 97, 104, 108, 109
criminal involvement, vii, x, 91, 106
criminal sentencing, 89
criminality, vii, viii, 1, 2, 3, 4, 5, 7, 8, 9, 27, 28, 29, 30, 31, 32, 33, 34, 35, 36, 37, 38, 39, 48, 49, 50, 51, 56, 59, 60, 61, 63, 65, 74, 78, 81, 83, 84, 85, 92, 93, 95
criminals, 4, 48, 50, 56, 58, 63, 64, 69, 78, 81, 84
criminology, vii, ix, x, 5, 41, 42, 44, 59, 65, 71, 91
crises, 55, 63, 64
cross-sectional study, 99
cues, 78, 84, 86
cultivation, 88
cultural norms, 94
culture, ix, 41, 44, 54, 59, 60, 61, 63, 76

D

danger, 83, 84
dangerousness, 78, 79, 81
data set, 103
deduction, 54

deformation, 37
degradation, 35
delinquency, 51, 58, 64, 92, 93, 94, 95, 98, 99, 105, 106, 107, 108, 110
delinquent behavior, 106
demographic characteristics, vii, ix, 33, 73, 81, 84
demography, 22
denial, 58
Department of Justice, 87
dependent variable, 60, 61, 80
depth, 110
detachment, 95, 96
detection, 78, 103, 107
deterrence, 61, 103, 104, 106, 107, 108, 109
developmental psychology, 93, 95
deviation, 3
diffusion, 6
discrimination, 75, 86, 87
diseases, 102
distinctness, 37
distortions, 103
distribution, 5, 53, 56, 57, 104, 105, 106, 111
diversity, 17
dopamine, 51
drawing, 93, 95
drug abuse, 51
Drug Enforcement Administration, 75

E

economic activity, 38
economic crisis, 21
economic development, viii, 2, 7, 8, 10, 14, 17, 19, 20, 21, 34, 35, 36
economic downturn, 56
economic growth, 17, 19, 35
economic indicator, 40
economics, viii, 1, 2, 5
education, 25, 26, 27, 58
EEG, 80
egalitarianism, 60
egocentrism, 48
egoism, 57, 60, 62, 63
e-mail, 41, 91
emitters, 80
emotional reactions, 80
empathy, 47, 48
empirical studies, 3
employees, 64
employers, 64
employment, 111
energy, 16, 44
enforcement, vii, 74, 76, 78, 81, 82, 83, 84, 86, 87, 88
entitlement, ix, 41, 44, 57
environment(s), 6, 47, 49, 50, 58, 63, 69, 70, 84, 95
environmental conditions, 46, 50, 53
environmental factors, 42, 47, 58, 60
environmental stimuli, 49, 50, 63, 78
equality, 77
ethnicity, 86, 88
etiology, 43, 61, 62, 97
evidence, 46, 87, 92, 97, 98, 110
evolution, 38, 43, 65, 67, 71
evolutionary psychologists, 45
excitability, 50
executive function, 69, 88
executive functioning, 69, 88
exercise, 49, 107, 108
exposure, 78
extinction, 45
extraction, 13

F

fear, 86, 87, 88, 89
federal courts, 71
feelings, 101, 102
femininity, 94
fidelity, 87
financial, 44, 63
fitness, 45, 46
food, 15, 16, 17
food industry, 16, 17
force, 5, 14, 57, 61
formation, 5, 14, 78, 87, 96, 108, 111
formula, 11

fragments, 4
fraud, 44, 45, 51, 52, 54, 56, 57, 60, 61, 62, 63, 64, 67, 68
freedom, 53
friendship, 49, 50

G

GABA, 50
gambling, 57
game theory, 43
gender, vii, ix, x, 73, 74, 77, 78, 80, 81, 82, 83, 84, 85, 87, 88, 89, 91, 92, 93, 94, 96, 97, 99, 103, 105, 106, 107, 108, 109, 110
gender differences, vii, 87, 93, 94, 97, 99, 108
gender effects, 88
gender gap, 92, 93, 96, 97, 106, 108, 109
gender role, 96
gene promoter, 65
generalizability, 108
genes, 42, 45, 47, 49, 50, 59, 60, 63
genetics, 43, 47, 50, 51, 58
genotype, 50
geography, 5
Georgia, 91
Germany, 114
goods and services, 61
governance, 54
grades, 99
graduate education, 10, 25, 26, 27, 28
graffiti, 101, 102
growth, 6, 7, 8, 17, 21, 22, 29, 33, 34, 35, 36, 37
growth rate, 35, 36, 37
guilt, 47, 48

H

health, 7, 10, 21, 22, 23, 24, 51
health problems, 51
heart rate, 43
higher education, 10, 25, 26, 27, 28
history, 5, 42, 50
hormones, 42
hot spots, vii, 1
human, 6, 7, 8, 35, 36, 43, 46, 47, 56, 75, 79
human agency, 56, 75
human behavior, 43
human capital, 6, 7, 8, 35, 36
human nature, 43, 46
hypothesis, 3, 7, 38, 62, 74

I

ideal, 75, 110
identification, vii, viii, 1, 2, 3, 7, 75, 86, 88, 95
illusory correlation, 78, 87, 88
image, 96
imbalances, 8
imitation, 59
impulsivity, 48, 95, 101
incarceration, 65, 96
incidence, 61
income, 49, 57, 58
independence, 96
independent variable, 106
individual character, 55
individuals, 43, 44, 45, 46, 47, 48, 49, 50, 51, 54, 55, 57, 59, 60, 61, 76, 77, 80, 81, 84, 86
industrial sectors, 14
industry(s), 9, 13, 14, 15, 16, 21, 43, 53, 57, 61, 62, 64
ineffectiveness, 34
infant mortality, 10, 21, 22, 24, 35
infants, 10, 95
inferences, 109
inflation, 61, 63, 64
infrastructure, 6, 7, 9, 11, 12
inheritance, 58, 60
institutions, 61
integration, ix, 41, 42, 63, 104
intelligence, 58
internal consistency, 103
internalization, 78
intervention, 74, 85
intervention strategies, 85

intimacy, 53
investment(s), 10, 17, 18, 19, 20, 21, 34
investors, 19, 21
Iowa, 73
Irkutsk Region, viii, 2
iron, 13, 14
IRS, 57
issues, 69, 86

J

justification, 59
juvenile delinquency, 93, 96, 98, 106, 109

K

kinship, 45
Krasnodar region, viii, 2
Kurgan Region, viii, 2

L

later life, 96
law enforcement, ix, 61, 74, 75, 76, 80
laws, 5, 7, 8
lead, 44, 53, 61, 63, 77, 83, 93, 95
learning, 49, 58, 110
lens, 87
level of education, 10
life course, 42, 66
life expectancy, 10, 21, 22, 24
life quality, 37
lifetime, 65
light, 102
Likert scale, 101, 102, 103
linear model, 105, 107, 109
liquidity, 44, 61
litigation, 75
living conditions, 102
love, 47, 102
loyalty, 46, 54

M

Machiavellianism, 61
machinery, 3, 6
magnitude, 49, 50, 59, 60, 107
majority, 49, 50, 56, 58, 64, 78
majority group, 78
manipulation, 53
manufacturing, 13, 53
masculinity, 94, 96
mass, 96
maternal control, 98
matter, 45
measurement, 108
media, 67, 82
membership, 76
mental ability, 87
mental life, 43
methodology, ix, 2
middle class, 58, 71
migration, 5, 6, 7, 9, 14, 16, 17, 19
minorities, 78
minority groups, 78
misconceptions, 71
models, ix, 47, 48, 74, 83, 93, 97, 106, 107
moral beliefs, 106, 107, 108
morality, 56, 102, 108
mortality, 10, 22, 23, 24, 51
mortality rate, 22, 23, 24, 51
Moscow, 11, 12, 14, 16, 19, 33, 34, 39, 40
motivation, 45
multiplier, 104
multi-stage sampling, 99, 103

N

narcissism, 57
National Research Council, 86
natural advantages, 17
natural selection, 60
negative consequences, 6, 110
neglect, 48, 95
neurons, 42
neuroscience, 43

neurotransmitter(s), 50, 51, 52
New Zealand, 68
norepinephrine, 51
normal distribution, 50

O

offenders, 51, 55, 56, 57, 58, 60, 61, 62, 63, 64, 71
officials, 75
oil, 16
operant conditioning, 58
opportunities, 17, 19, 20, 38, 44, 54, 55, 56, 57, 60, 61, 62, 63
organism, 4, 39, 44, 45, 49
organize, 59
oversight, ix, 41, 44, 54, 55, 56, 61, 62, 63

P

Pacific, 69
parallel, 102
parental control, 94, 98
parenting, 47, 49, 50, 95, 97, 98, 109
parents, 47, 51, 94, 95, 96, 97, 99, 107, 110
participants, 79, 80
path model, 104, 105, 106
pathways, 106, 110
performers, 26
permit, 34, 49
personality, 58, 60, 61, 65, 108, 111
personality traits, 58, 60, 65
personality type, 61
pharmacological treatment, 50
phenotype(s), 42, 49, 50, 52, 53
physical interaction, 54
plants, 19
plasticity, 46
platform, 4
police, vii, ix, 73, 74, 75, 76, 77, 78, 79, 80, 81, 82, 83, 84, 85, 86, 87, 88
police-citizen encounters, ix, 73, 74, 76, 82
policy, 34, 61, 64, 88
politics, 61
polymorphism, 49, 65
population, ix, 3, 6, 7, 8, 9, 10, 12, 13, 14, 15, 16, 21, 22, 23, 24, 25, 26, 27, 28, 33, 34, 35, 36, 37, 38, 47, 49, 50, 51, 53, 60, 72, 73
population density, 9
population size, 9
population structure, 23, 27
poverty, 48
predictor variables, 105, 106, 107, 109
prestige, 77
prevention, 3, 36, 64
primary caregivers, x, 92, 94, 96, 106, 108
principles, 39, 86
probability, 3
profit, 46
property crimes, 103
proposition, 108
proteins, 49
psychological processes, ix, 74, 75
psychology, 43, 45, 63, 65, 68, 74, 79, 83
psychopaths, 47, 48, 55, 57, 58, 62, 63, 64
psychopathy, 65, 71
Puerto Rico, 99
punishment, 50, 89, 95, 103

Q

quality improvement, 35
quality of life, 8
questionnaire, 100

R

race, vii, ix, 51, 73, 74, 75, 76, 77, 78, 79, 80, 81, 82, 83, 84, 85, 87, 88, 89
racism, 78
raw materials, 21
reactions, 4
reality, 85
recall, 36
recession, 63, 64
reciprocity, 46, 53, 57
recognition, 97, 110

reforms, 56, 63
regression, viii, 2, 51, 104, 105, 106, 107, 108, 109
regression analysis, viii, 2
regression model, 107, 108
regression weights, 104
regulations, 60
reimburse, 45
reinforcement, 59, 60
rejection, 95
relatives, 45
relevance, 5
remorse, 48
representativeness, 103
reproduction, 7, 10, 43, 47, 52, 53
reproductive age, 49
Republic of Buryatia, viii, 2
reputation, 87
requirements, 14
researchers, 5, 75, 79, 108
resilience, ix, 41, 44
resources, 44, 45, 54, 57, 61, 82, 84
response, 4, 79, 80, 87, 95, 100
rhetoric, 89
risk(s), 48, 49, 50, 52, 53, 56, 57, 61, 82, 87, 94, 95, 96, 101, 103, 107
risk factors, 49
risk perception, 94, 95
risk-taking, 48, 95, 96, 101
RNA, 49
root(s), 4, 38, 64
rules, 43, 53, 59, 63
rural areas, 17
rural population, viii, 2
Russia, viii, 1, 2, 12, 30, 33, 39, 40

S

schema, 78
school, 99, 100, 102, 103
school authority, 103
science, 10, 25, 26, 27, 28, 39, 65, 66
scientific theory, ix, 41, 44
scope, 81
security, 54
self-control, vii, x, 42, 48, 58, 67, 91, 92, 93, 94, 95, 96, 97, 98, 99, 101, 104, 105, 106, 107, 108, 109, 111
self-employed, 58
self interest, 45, 57
sensations, 50
sensitivity, 110
serotonin, 51
service industries, 53
settlements, 16, 19
sex, 42, 106, 109
shade, 35
shame, 47
shape, vii, ix, 73, 76
shoot, 79, 80, 83, 87
showing, 44
siblings, 50
significance level, 103
signs, 17
simulation(s), 79, 87
skeleton, 34
skin, 43
social behavior, 47
social behaviour, 67
social capital, 34
social cognition, 88
social context, 59, 84
social contract, 46
social control, viii, 1, 39, 46, 53, 54, 64
social development, 8, 32
social exchange, 46, 47
social interaction, 86
social learning, 44, 59
social life, 3, 4
social reality, 4, 111
social relations, 52, 53
social sciences, vii, ix, 73
social status, 44, 76, 81, 82, 83, 84
social structure, 80
social welfare, 37
socialization, 59, 93, 94, 96, 97
society, 3, 38, 39, 47, 48, 53, 60, 61, 64, 77, 81, 92, 96
sociology, 43, 74
sociopath, 47, 48, 57, 63

solidarity, 46
solution, 5
specialists, 3, 9
species, 45
St. Petersburg, 12, 19, 33
stability, 14, 102, 111
stabilization, 8, 34
standard error, 103
standardized testing, 77
state(s), 4, 7, 8, 10, 21, 22, 23, 24, 38, 39, 53, 54, 67, 77, 81, 82, 83, 84, 86, 95, 89
statistics, 10, 23, 29, 31, 38, 92
steel, 13, 14
steel industry, 13, 14
stereotypes, 78, 79, 80, 84, 85, 87
stereotyping, 78, 87, 88
stratification, 88, 100, 103
stress, 52
structure, vii, ix, 1, 3, 5, 8, 9, 16, 17, 19, 23, 26, 27, 36, 37, 42, 43, 44, 47, 50, 54, 55, 60, 61, 103
style, 102, 111
substance abuse, 51
supervision, 94, 95, 97, 98
surplus, 49, 56, 104
surveillance, 54
survival, 43
Sverdlovsk oblast, viii, 2
Sweden, 41, 51, 57, 71
sympathy, 47
synthesis, vii, ix, 41, 43

T

tactics, 75
target, 74, 76, 80, 81, 82, 83, 84, 97
tax evasion, 57, 71
tax system, 57
taxation, 57
teachers, 100
techniques, 7, 48, 59, 67, 97, 109
tension, 4
territorial, viii, 1, 2, 3, 4, 5, 7, 8, 9, 12, 38, 39
territory, 3, 4, 5, 6, 8, 14, 17, 19, 36
tertiary sector, 14
test scores, 87
testing, 7, 9, 64, 85, 93
thoughts, 101, 102
threats, 17
thrill-seeking, ix, 41, 44, 55
traffic stops, 75, 80, 85, 88
training, 79, 80
traits, 47, 76, 80, 81, 85, 94, 110
transactions, 53
Transbaikal region, viii, 2
transformation, 3, 35
transport, 6, 12, 14
transport costs, 6
treatment, 50, 52
triggers, 50

U

Ukraine, 12
unconscious processes, 79
uniform, 5
United States, 75
universities, 26, 27
updating, 42
urban, 9, 11, 14, 17, 36, 39
urban agglomerations, 9, 36
urban population, 9, 11, 14, 17
urban settlement, 9, 17
urbanization, 5, 7
USA, 65
USSR, 3

V

variables, 42, 102, 103, 104, 106
variations, 98
vector, 6, 7, 8, 14, 17, 21, 35, 37
versatility, 101, 104, 105
violence, 51
violent crime, 60, 103
violent offenders, 51
Volkswagen, 19
Voronezh Regions, viii, 2, 22

vulnerability, 96

W

war, 81
Washington, 86, 87, 111
wealth, 76
weapons, 80, 87, 88
websites, 10
well-being, 34, 36, 38
Western Europe, 12
white collar crime, vii, ix, 41, 42, 43, 44, 51, 52, 56, 57, 61
witnesses, 81
workers, 61
wrongdoing, 102

Y

Yale University, 70, 112
yield, 93
young people, 82